On Your Bike

HAMPSHIRE & THE NEW FOREST

Mike Edwards

COUNTRYSIDE BOOKS
NEWBURY BERKSHIRE

COUNTRYSIDE BOOKS
3 Catherine Road
Newbury, Berkshire

To view our complete range of books,
please visit us at
www.countrysidebooks.co.uk

ISBN 978 1 84674 268 2

For Anne-Marie

Designed by Peter Davies, Nautilus Design
Maps by Jennie Collins
Photographs by the author

Produced through MRM Associates Ltd., Reading
Typeset by CJWT Solutions, St Helens
Printed in India

CONTENTS

AREA MAP SHOWING THE LOCATIONS OF THE RIDES

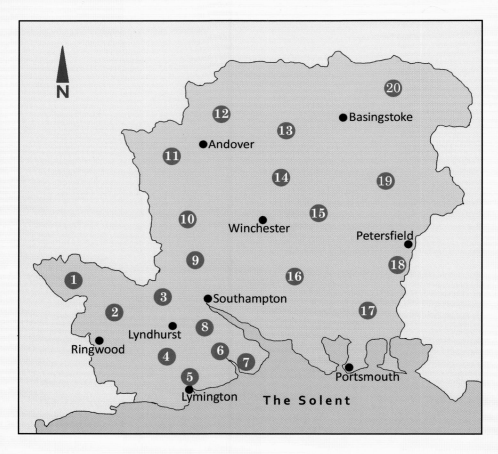

INTRODUCTION

O n your bike you are free to explore Hampshire's wealth of glorious countryside and discover some of the secrets of less-frequented areas. You can enjoy spectacular views from the more remote hills of the South Downs, take your time following the county's lush river valleys through old-world villages of cob, flint and thatch, and meander at your leisure through the still medieval landscape of the New Forest.

But Hampshire has much more than its unrivalled network of quiet lanes and beautiful countryside to offer. Man has settled this attractive county since prehistoric times and has left a rich legacy for you to enjoy along the routes of these rides. You can step back into the Iron Age with a visit to Danebury Hill Fort and the recreated Iron Age village at Butser Hill, and follow the legions along the Devil's Highway to Silchester Roman Town. As well as its famous Motor Museum you can find a stately home built from the ruins of a 12th-century abbey at Beaulieu in the New Forest. Elizabethan mansions include Breamore in the Avon valley and The Vyne, north of Basingstoke. Recall the canal era by following the towpath beside the Basingstoke Canal and the coming of the railways as you ride along the trackbeds of former lines. The restored Mid-Hants Railway between Alresford and Alton features on two of these tours and all the family will enjoy a trip on the little steam railway in Lord Rothschild's Exbury Gardens. An interesting ride traces the course of a Civil War battle when Roundhead faced Cavalier on the downs near Cheriton, and other routes recall wartime days as they run past the military airfields at Lymington and Odiham, and follow the beach at Lepe to the dock where parts of the Mulberry Harbour were constructed. The Museum of Army Flying is close to one of these rides.

There are opportunities to visit some of Hampshire's most fascinating rarities such as Britain's only working silk mill – at Whitchurch on the River Test – and the Sammy Miller Motorcycle Museum. Standing alone in a field high on the downs near the tiny village of Crux Easton you will find a fully-restored, 19th-century wind engine. Time to relax? Beautiful gardens are a feature of the Hampshire countryside and the rides include the wonderful rose garden at Mottisfont and the New Forest garden at Furzey, which contains a 400-year-old cob cottage. And who could resist a break in one of the many pubs and tearooms mentioned along the way?

In this book I have tried to include routes that have given me a great deal of pleasure and are suitable for leisure cyclists. I hope you will enjoy them as much as I did and may you spend many happy days exploring my home county.

Mike Edwards

GUIDE TO USING THIS BOOK

Each route is preceded by information to help you:

The **introduction** describes the special appeal of the countryside chosen for the ride, gives brief details of the route and mentions some of the interesting features you will see on the way.

The **sketch maps** accompanying each ride give you a general idea of the route but can provide only limited information. It is well worthwhile to purchase the appropriate **map(s)** listed in the text from the Ordnance Survey Landranger 1:50 000 series and, if possible, take the relevant OS 1:25 000 Explorer map(s) with you for more detail.

The grid reference of the suggested **starting point** is given but you can start from any convenient point on the route.

Some places for **refreshment** are indicated in the text but you are sure to find your favourites as Hampshire has plenty of tempting pubs and cafés.

The note on the **route** is intended to guide you in your choice of tour. Only a few of the rides include hilly sections.

THE ROUTES
Route descriptions are kept simple.

Changes of direction are printed in bold type: **turn L**, **turn R**. In some of the more remote country areas turnings may not be signed so I have used other means, such as road names, as guides.

Many of the routes include off-road sections which simply mean a bridleway, towpath or other track where you shouldn't encounter motor vehicles – ideal for those first outings with children.

If you haven't taken the children cycling before, the most important thing to remember is that the outing must be a pleasure for every member of the family. Keep the early rides short; let yourself be persuaded to go a little further next time! You will be surprised how quickly even the youngest cyclist improves and how rapidly his range increases. Choose a quiet route to begin with – a towpath or a bridleway is ideal – and let the slowest member of the family set the pace. Nobody should ever be left behind to struggle on alone!

You can usually shorten or lengthen most of these rides, if necessary, using the OS maps.

SAFETY TIPS
Join the Cyclists' Touring Club. The third-party insurance, which is free to members, makes this a

no-brainer on its own! Visit their website www.ctc.org.uk or telephone 01483 417217.

Carry your kit on your bike, not on your back. Rear pannier bags are best for heavy items, perhaps with a detachable handlebar bag with a shoulder strap to take in with you on café stops.

Don't be lured into using uncomfortable racing clothes or equipment. There are no prizes, so choose a comfortable bike and wear fairly loose clothes to suit the conditions. Several layers are preferable to a single thick garment, and shoes in particular need to be chosen with care. I do recommend a proper pair of cycling shorts or trousers lined with chamois leather – they are great for preventing saddle-soreness on a long ride. A waterproof, windproof, breathable, high-visibility jacket is also an excellent investment. It can be supplemented with an extra layer or two in cold weather, and a light pair of waterproof over-trousers completes the outfit.

Get your bike fitted with low gears suitable for touring and load-carrying. It is less tiring to pedal at a higher rate, rather than strain to force the pedals round.

Keep your heels well back when pedalling so that your ankles become part of your pedalling action too. Watch where an experienced cyclist puts his feet on the pedals. If you use toe-clips or clip-in cycling shoes, you will guarantee the proper pedalling action.

Reduce drag by keeping tyres pumped up to their proper recommended pressures. You can find this on the tyre wall. Often it is around 65 psi for a touring bike, and you will need a good pump to reach it.

A rear-view mirror is just as necessary to the bike-rider as it is to the motorist. I use a Bike-Eye, which attaches to the frame and eliminates vibration, but even a helmet mirror is a great help.

Full-size wheels are more comfortable and safer than tiny ones, and mudguards only weigh a few ounces and save a lot of laundry bills. Get a quick lesson on how to mend a puncture, and equip yourself with a set of tyre levers, a repair kit, and a few simple cycle tools.

Get a 3-way Allen Key from a cycle shop. You only need one to adjust all the family bikes, and it is worth carrying it with you on long journeys as it should fit all the adjustment points on a modern bike.

Buy a lady's shower-cap from Boots the Chemist. It's ideal to put over the saddle when taking a break from a rainstorm.

Carry a good supply of an isotonic sports drink; this replaces the salts in your body, as well as the liquid. You can save cash by making your own – just Google 'Sports Drink'.

Don't listen to music whilst cycling – you can't hear the traffic warnings or greetings from other cyclists. Listen to the sounds of the countryside instead.

And I have kept my best tip for last. Get a copy of *The Bike Book* (Haynes), which covers bike maintenance, and *The Long Distance Cyclists' Handbook* by Simon Doughty (A. & C. Black), which deals with every other aspect of riding a bike with infectious enthusiasm!

ACKNOWLEDGEMENTS

It is a pleasure to acknowledge the generous help and advice I have received in writing this book. Chris Juden, CTC Senior Technical Officer, started the wheels turning by guiding me to my beloved Gazelle Fuente off-road bike on which I completed many of these tours. Jackie Garratt encouraged me by exploring some of the remote places suggested on the Solent shore, and Captain Dick Snell and his wife Liz were always ready with technical advice and assistance. Paula Leigh and Deb Marshman at Countryside Books were ready to help at all times. And as ever, my wife Anne-Marie and our daughter Julie never failed to keep me afloat on the many occasions when I needed support.

Across the Avon to Rockbourne and Damerham

20 miles

This tour leaves the wide heaths and dense woods of the New Forest and takes you west across the Avon valley to follow quiet lanes meandering over rolling downland, threaded by fertile river valleys – attractive countryside that has attracted settlers since earliest times. Starting from Fordingbridge the route leads to Breamore where Saxon tribes built a church, little changed today. Nearby stands Breamore House, an Elizabethan mansion. High on the downs, offering glorious views, you reach Whitsbury hill fort dating back to the Iron Age. You then run down into a beautiful valley to discover Rockbourne, a streamside village with thatched, timber-framed houses. Close by are the fascinating remains of a Roman villa. You ride through Damerham – another charming old world village – before returning along more downland lanes to Fordingbridge.

Maps: OS Landranger 195 Bournemouth & Purbeck and 184 Salisbury & The Plain.

Starting point: Fordingbridge long-stay car park (not shown on OS map).

Travelling north on the A338 take the exit for Fordingbridge on the slip road. The car park is immediately on your right. Southbound on the A338 take the exit slip road for Fordingbridge, drive under the A338 and turn immediately left (GR 151140).

By train: No convenient station.

Refreshments: Pubs in all the villages. I recommend for cyclists the Cartwheel at Whitsbury. Tearooms in Fordingbridge and Breamore. Alderholt Mill is open and serves teas weekends and bank holidays from Easter between 2 pm and 6 pm.

The route: A generally easy undulating route.

From the car park **turn R** along the B3078 for Godshill. At first the road crosses the flat farmlands of the Avon valley but then the scenery changes dramatically as it runs uphill and bears left, signed Brook, to cross the western boundary of the New Forest at Godshill. **Turn L** just before you reach the Fighting Cocks pub, signed Woodgreen. The lane runs downhill into the valley of the Millersford stream past an alpaca farm on the left.

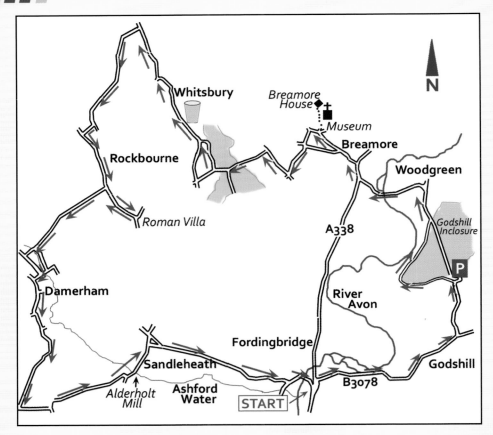

Across the stream the lane rises to a Y-junction. **Turn L**, signed Castle Hill, and follow the narrow lane as it traces the hillside then curves right to follow the edge of a steep cliff with magnificent views west over the Avon valley. This is an ideal place to enjoy a picnic or a snack on one of the seats overlooking the river, which winds like a silver ribbon through the meadows below you.

Continue to a T-junction. **Turn L** to ride downhill into Woodgreen village. At the next T-junction **turn L**, signed Breamore. Cross the bridges over the Avon and follow the road past the mill

to meet the A338. **Turn R**, signed Salisbury. Pass the village shop on your left and a few yards further on **turn L**, signed Breamore. The lane runs over Breamore Common. When the lane curves sharp left, leave it and keep straight on, passing a house on your left. Cross a lane and follow the sign for Breamore church. A visit to this 10th-century church is a must!

Return past the drive to Breamore House and follow the sign for the excellent Countryside Museum and Tea Barn. After your visit **turn R** from the Tea Barn and **turn R** again opposite the drive to Breamore House. At the

Looking west over the Avon Valley from Castle Hill

crossroads **turn R**, signed Whitsbury. When the lane curves left keep straight on, signed Whitsbury, to a crossroads. **Turn R**, signed Whitsbury. The lane turns sharp left and climbs through woods to a Y-junction. **Turn R**, still following the Whitsbury sign, to a T-junction where you **turn R** to ride into Whitsbury village.

Continue uphill. The road bears left then right past a stud farm, then curves left for Rockbourne and Damerham. You are now high up on the downs and you enjoy a splendid downhill run to a T-junction. **Turn L**, signed Rockbourne, and ride through this attractive village; follow the brown sign for Rockbourne Roman villa. The villa entrance is on your right.

After your visit retrace your route as far as a lane on your left signed Damerham. **Turn L**, signed Damerham and Cranborne. Continue for 1¼ miles, then cross a stream to a T-junction.

Turn L along High Street, signed Fordingbridge. Shortly you reach another T-junction. (The sign indicates a left turn for Fordingbridge, but I prefer a longer, more attractive route.) So **turn R**, signed Cranborne and Primary School. After a short distance **turn L**, signed Crendell and Lower Daggons. Continue for about 1½ miles to a T-junction. A sign indicates the lane you are following from Damerham (2½ miles) and the lane on the right for Cranborne (4½ miles). Although there is no sign, **turn L**, passing a small iron-railed bridge on your left.

The lane runs for 1¼ miles to a T-junction. **Turn L**, signed Sandleheath, Fordingbridge and Rockbourne. Continue past Alderholt Mill to a T-junction. **Turn R**, signed Fordingbridge. Keep ahead for 2 miles, following the sign for Fordingbridge, to ride through the town to a traffic island. **Turn R**, signed B3078 Ringwood, cross the

A welcoming picnic spot by the River Avon at Fordingbridge

bridge over the Avon and **turn R**, following the sign for the Sports Ground and long-stay car park.

BREAMORE HOUSE

The mansion was completed in 1583 by William Doddington, Auditor of the Tower Mint. Later the house and estate were sold to George II's physician, Sir Edward Hulse, and it is still the Hulse family home. Inside you will find a splendid collection of furniture and paintings. Opening times are from 2 pm to 5.30 pm (last guided tour 4.30 pm) on Tuesday and Sunday during April. From May to September the house is open all week except Friday and Saturday. Telephone: 01725 512858.

COUNTRYSIDE MUSEUM

The museum is open on the same days as Breamore House from 1 pm to 5.30 pm and the Tea Barn from 12 midday to 5.30 pm.

BREAMORE CHURCH

Much of the Saxon fabric of this ancient church survives, showing typical 'long and short' work and deep-splayed round-topped windows. Above the south door is a Saxon sculpture and there is an inscription in Anglo-Saxon on the arch leading into the south transept translated as 'here is made plain the covenant to thee'.

ROCKBOURNE ROMAN VILLA

The villa, with forty-two rooms, is one of the largest discovered in southern Britain. Among its many interesting features are two stunning mosaic floors and a unique form of underfloor heating. Call in at the museum to discover more of the site's history, which spans the period from the Iron Age to the 5th century AD. Open from early April to the end of September on Tuesday, Wednesday, Thursday and Sunday from 11 am to 4 pm. Telephone: 08456 035635.

2
Fritham and the Avon Valley

18 miles

A magnificent ride along a high ridge giving wonderful views over the west of the Forest must be the highlight of this tour. But there is much more to enjoy. You visit Eyeworth Pond, one of the most beautiful places in the Forest, discover some of the secrets of the Forest's wartime airfields and follow a quiet lane winding along the Avon valley, past old world farms and cottages. The tour starts in Fritham, a remote village at the end of a lane that disappears into the Forest. Set among wide greens where animals roam freely and surrounded by oak and beech woods rich in wildlife, this little place is a delight in all seasons.

Map: OS Landranger 195 Bournemouth & Purbeck.

Starting point: Fritham car park. The easiest way to Fritham by car is to take the minor road, the B3079, for Brook and Bramshaw, at the Cadnam roundabout. Just past the Bell Inn in Brook, follow the B3078 for Fordingbridge. After about 1½ miles turn left for Fritham. Take the second turning on the right to drive through the village past the Royal Oak inn and turn left into the car park (GR 231141).

By train: No convenient station.

Refreshments: This ride is the thirsty cyclist's dream! Apart from the Royal Oak at Fritham, you pass the following pubs: the High Corner Inn, the Red Shoot Inn, the Alice Lisle near Moyles Court, the Royal Oak at North Gorley and the Foresters at Frogham.

The route: Quiet country lanes and forest tracks. The route is undulating with some short, fairly steep climbs.

Turn L from the car park entrance to the road leading downhill. On the corner stands an old black iron post box. Nowhere could look more peaceful today but during the 19th century this part of the Forest was the centre of a thriving industry. The Schultze gunpowder works flourished at Eyeworth at the foot of the hill. The post box was placed on the top of the hill out of consideration for the postman!

As you come down the hill Eyeworth Pond sparkles through the trees a little to your right. Clouds of oaks and beeches clothe the hillside beyond. **Turn R** with the pond on your left. Now an idyllic scene and a haven for wildlife, the pond was constructed as a

13

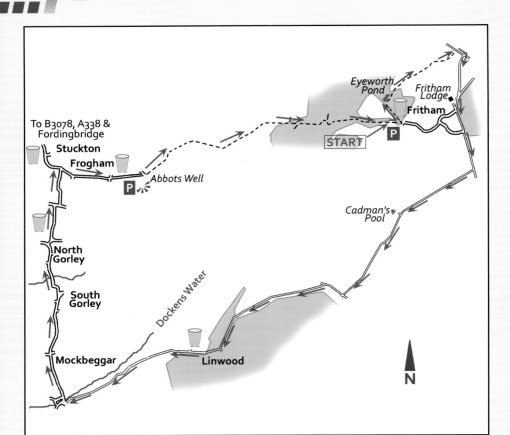

reservoir to supply the huge amount of water required by the gunpowder works.

Continue past the barrier along the track into woodland. Originally this was known as Powder Mill Road. It was cut from Eyeworth to the present B3078 to take the carts laden with containers of gunpowder, which, as the works prospered, became too heavy for the horses to pull up the hill to Fritham. After 100 yards look for a circle of wooden palings on your left surrounding the rust-coloured water of Irons Well. Follow the valley for 1½ miles to the B3078. **Turn R** for 200

yards then **turn R** again, signed Fritham, Bolderwood and Linwood. Continue over the open heathland to a junction. **Turn R**, signed Fritham. A track on your right leads to the impressive entrance of Fritham Lodge. After a mile **turn R**, signed Linwood and Bolderwood, to ride over the former wartime airfield of Stoney Cross.

The road stretches straight ahead of you over the moor, forming an ideal runway. A plane could take off on it still, especially as the road points into the prevailing south-westerly wind. Make a short detour and turn into the next car park on the right to see

The ridge ride to Fritham

Cadman's Pool, a hidden Forest gem. Continue over the moor to a T-junction. **Turn R**, signed Linwood. You pass a track on the right for High Corner Inn, a perfect refuelling stop.

The scenery changes dramatically as the road runs downhill through oak and birch woods past the Red Shoot Inn before winding through undulating countryside and finally descending to a junction in the Avon valley. **Turn R**, signed Mockbeggar and North Gorley, to cross the ford over Dockens Water. The large house on your left, now a school, is Moyles Court, once the home of a New Forest heroine, Alice Lisle. After the defeat of the Duke of

Monmouth's army at Sedgemoor, two wounded supporters of Monmouth were discovered exhausted in her garden. Although she was a Royalist and her husband was fighting for the king she sheltered and nursed the wounded men. For this humane act the notorious Judge Jeffreys ordered her to be beheaded. The gallant old lady died maintaining she was no traitor.

The road leads along the valley. After 1½ miles, through a gateway on your left you will see the former control tower of another wartime airfield, at Ibsley. A little further on, as you approach some houses, look left for the memorial to all who gave their lives. It

Waiting for opening time outside the Foresters pub

was erected by the RAF Ibsley Historical Group. Also inscribed on the memorial is a map of the airfield and an account of the part Ibsley played in the war.

Continue ahead at the junction, signed Fordingbridge, through South and North Gorley. Ignore the lane on the right signed for Frogham and keep ahead past the Royal Oak Inn to a T-junction. **Turn R** for 100 yards then **turn L**, signed Stuckton. After ½ mile **turn R**, signed Frogham. The road climbs steeply past the Foresters pub. At the top of the hill **turn R** into the unmarked car park to enjoy a magnificent view over the western Forest. The white bee-hived

shaped monument marks the millennium.

Ride down the hill. At the foot is Abbots Well, a perpetual spring first mentioned in the 13th century. The spring has two outlets, one open for animals and the other roofed for humans. Pass the barrier and take the marked cycle track over the Forest for Fritham. This splendid track leads you back to your car. The Royal Oak pub waits to welcome you.

● ●

THE SCHULTZE GUNPOWDER FACTORY
A whole factory complex was built at Eyeworth producing sporting powder

used for shooting game, hares and rabbits. In a booklet published in 1896 the Schultze Company boasted it was 'the premier Nitro-Compound Gunpowder Factory in the World'! Over 100 men were employed, often walking to work from as far afield as Downton, Redlynch and Fordingbridge. Sixty large buildings included shooting galleries and laboratories. The works were closed in 1910 when the last of the original three leases expired.

STONEY CROSS AIRFIELD

Work commenced at Stoney Cross in 1942. During the autumn and winter of 1943 preparations began for the D-Day landings and an American unit on the airfield assembled American-built Waco CG4 A gliders shipped in crates across the Atlantic. All this changed in 1944 with the arrival of the 367th Fighter Group USAAF who used Stoney Cross as a base for their P38 Lightning twin-engined aircraft in operations over France. The build-up for D-Day continued and, on 6th June, the Lightnings acted as low support for the Allied landings. Losses were considerable but the attacks went on until the group moved to Ibsley early in July. The airfield closed in 1945. *They Flew From the Forest* by Alan Brown gives a fascinating account of the Forest's wartime airfields. The book is published by EON Graphics, Highcliffe.

Eyeworth Pond

The Living Forest

22 miles

The New Forest is a very special place. For a thousand years people have lived and worked in this often still medieval landscape, creating a forest unlike any other. This ride combines beautiful scenery with some of the Forest's story, both today and in the past. The route starts near Lyndhurst, the Forest's capital. You take a winding road through ancient woodland to Bolderwood where you can watch wild deer being called out of the Forest by the keeper to be fed. The route then runs over high moorland, with splendid views to Nomansland on the Wiltshire border. A different aspect of Forest life is revealed as you cross Penn Common with its scattered farmsteads and heavily grazed grassland. More quiet lanes bring you back to your car after a visit to a delightful garden where you will find a 400-year-old cob cottage, typical of the Forest in the past. It has only two tiny bedrooms but it once housed a family of fourteen children!

Maps: OS Landranger 195 Bournemouth & Purbeck and 196 The Solent and Isle of Wight.

Starting point: Swan Green car park. Leave Lyndhurst on the A35, heading west for Bournemouth. After ½ mile, opposite the Swan pub, turn right for Emery Down. Cross the cattle grid and turn immediately left into Swan Green car park (GR 290082).

By train: Ashurst (New Forest) station is 2 miles north-east of Lyndhurst.

Refreshments: Tearooms in Lyndhurst, Minstead village shop and Furzey Gardens. Lyndhurst has a choice of pubs and on the route pubs include the Swan, the Lamb at Nomansland and the Trusty Servant at Minstead.

The route: The whole route runs through the Forest along quiet roads and lanes. No steep hills.

Turn L from Swan Green car park uphill to ride through Emery Down, an attractive village tucked in a wooded valley. By the New Forest Inn **turn L**, signed Bolderwood. After following this beautiful wooded road for a mile, over the grass on your left you will see the Portuguese Fireplace. During the First World War, Portuguese soldiers camped here to help the local forestry workers and the fireplace from their cookhouse was restored as a memorial to them.

Continue for another 2 miles to Bolderwood car park. Short waymarked walks lead from here and there is a surprising amount to discover, including an arboretum and

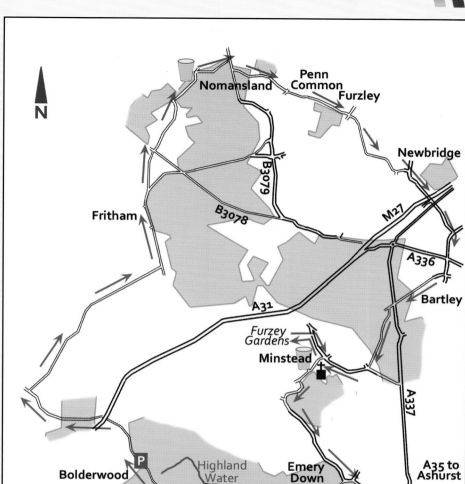

Bolderwood Farm deer sanctuary. One very cold winter the local keeper put food out for the deer and cared for any sick animals. Now they have been coming to Bolderwood for so long that they know instinctively they are safe.

Keep ahead, signed Fritham and Linwood, for ¼ mile and on your right you will see the Canadian Cross flanked by white flag poles. Behind the cross are two maple trees and beyond them pine woods slope steeply down into the valley of Highland Water. During the build up for D-Day, services were held here for the men of the 3rd

19

Wild deer at Bolderwood

Canadian Division and a yearly service is still held at the Cross.

The road ahead leads you under the A31 to a junction. **Turn R**, signed Stoney Cross, and follow the straight road ahead over the former wartime airfield (see Route 2) for 3 miles to a T-junction. **Turn L**, signed Bramshaw and Fritham. Pass Fritham on your left and continue ahead, signed Bramshaw and Nomansland. At the Y-junction **turn L**, signed Nomansland and Godshill. Continue straight over the B3078, signed Landford and Nomansland. A steep descent and a climb bring you to the Lamb Inn in Nomansland. According to Forest legend the village owes its name to the fact that no one could decide whether it was in Hampshire or Wiltshire! Within the Forest boundaries it was possible to claim squatters' rights providing you could establish some sort of a home with a fireplace without the authorities seeing you. If it was decided that a squatter had made his home in Wiltshire where this ruling did not apply, he could be evicted. There must have been some sort of compromise as the front step of the Lamb is in Hampshire and the rest of the building in Wiltshire!

Opposite the Lamb **turn R** for ½ mile to the B3079. **Turn R** for 200 yards then **turn L**, signed Newbridge. The route crosses the open grassland of Penn Common grazed by the Commoners' animals. Continue past the farms and cottages to Furzley. Cross straight over a road, following the sign for Copythorne and Newbridge, and keep ahead over Furzley and Cadnam commons for 1 mile to Newbridge. **Turn R**, signed Copythorne and Winsor.

Go under the motorway and straight over the crossroads, signed Winsor. At the T-junction **turn R**, signed Cadnam and Bartley. Cross straight over the A336, following the sign for Bartley. At the crossroads by Bartley post office **turn R**, signed Minstead. In ¾ mile cross the A337 to a fork. Bear left, signed Minstead. At the T-junction **turn R** to ride into the village. Minstead church is so fascinating it demands a short detour! **Turn L** in front of the Trusty Servant Inn up the hill to the church. After your visit,

return to the Trusty Servant and **turn L** to continue uphill to pass the sign for Stoney Cross. Shortly **turn L** by Minstead village hall, following the brown sign for Furzey Gardens. The road leads to the entrance to the gardens on the left. This is a real Forest woodland garden, with a network of winding paths leading to a beautiful lake.

Retrace your route in the direction of Minstead, turning right at the T-junction by the village hall. Before you reach the village **turn R**, over a ford, signed Newtown and Fleetwater. **Turn L** along the first lane on the left (unsigned). Follow the lane to a T-junction. **Turn L** and continue along this road, which runs through Emery Down to Swan Green car park on your right.

Commoners' animals at Penn Common

MINSTEAD CHURCH

This homely little church is built of traditional Forest materials, wattle filled in with rubble and daub. Stone could only be spared for the arches and corners of the main walls. Inside there is a very rare three-decker pulpit and the family of nearby Castle Malwood House had their own private pew. It is more like a cosy sitting room with a fireplace and its own entrance from an outside staircase. Sir Arthur Conan Doyle lived in the parish and his grave is in the churchyard.

FURZEY GARDENS

The gardens, with their 400-year-old cottage, are open daily until dusk all year. Telephone: 02380 812464. There is also a gallery selling local arts and crafts, open daily from March to October from 10 am to 5 pm; its tearoom serves refreshments until 4.30 pm.

The grave of Sir Arthur Conan Doyle in Minstead churchyard

Around Burley and Brockenhurst

19 miles

Starting from Burley, a picturesque village in the heart of the New Forest, this ride takes you through some of the Forest's most enchanting scenery. After riding off-road through tranquil Inclosures, rich in wildlife, you turn down the Ornamental Drive near Lyndhurst to discover the Forest's oldest tree, the Knightwood Oak. This mighty tree has provided a home for the Purple Emperor butterfly for over 350 years. Continuing through Brockenhurst you pass the village's ancient church and follow quiet country lanes to the start of an exhilarating five-mile ride along the embanked track of the railway that once ran across the Forest to Dorchester. A short ride brings you back to Burley.

Maps: OS Landranger 195 Bournemouth & Purbeck and 196 The Solent & Isle of Wight. The Forestry Commission and National Park Authority publish a map showing off-road Forest cycle routes – obtainable from Information Centres.

Starting point: The 24-hour public car park (pay-and-display) adjoining the Queen's Head car park in Burley (GR 212031).

By train: Brockenhurst station.

Refreshments: Pubs and tearooms in Burley and Brockenhurst. The Station House is now a tearoom and I can recommend the Forest Tea House on the right as you approach Burley for excellent cream teas and homemade cakes.

The route: An easy flat route combining scenic Forest tracks with quiet country lanes.

Turn L from the car park entrance down Chapel Lane. Over the parkland on your left you have a fine view of Burley Manor. It is possible a manor has stood on this site since before the Conquest. It was once the home of Sir Simon de Burley, tutor to the Black Prince. Sir Simon was executed in the Tower of London for alleged treason. The Manor is now a hotel.

Follow the lane past Woods Corner and uphill for a mile to approach a sharp right-hand bend. Do not continue round the turn but keep straight on along a gravel track passing Anderwood Cottage, dated 1876, on your left to go through the gate into Anderwood Inclosure. Follow the waymarked cycle track as it winds its way through beautiful oak woods to a T-junction. **Turn R** and continue through a

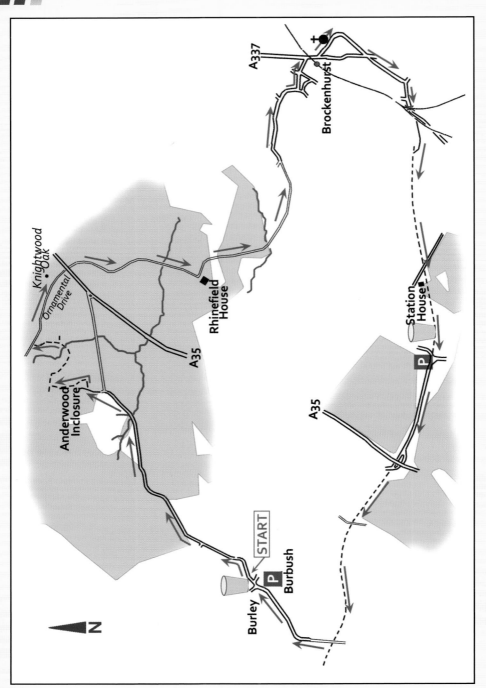

A charming corner of Burley village

gate. Keep straight on at a junction to go past a barrier and meet the Bolderwood branch of the Ornamental Drive.

Turn R to follow this lovely way to the Knightwood Oak. The path to the oak leads from the Drive on your left. The Knightwood Oak is 100 ft tall and 23 ft all the way round. This kingly tree is now the centre of the aptly-named 'Monarch's Grove'. To mark the ninth centenary of the New Forest in 1979, HM The Queen and the Duke of Edinburgh planted an oak nearby and eighteen oaks were planted a short distance away to represent all the recorded visits of reigning monarchs to the New Forest from William I to Edward VII in 1903.

Continue to the A35, cross straight over and ride down Rhinefield Ornamental Drive through totally different scenery! This southern branch of the Drive originally formed the approach to Rhinefield House, once the home of the Master Keeper of the Forest, now a luxury hotel. The Drive forms an avenue of exotic trees, most of which were planted in 1859. Among them you will see redwoods, home for the tiny goldcrest. To enjoy more of this unique area stop off in Blackwater car park and follow some of the short marked trails.

The route leaves the trees, crosses Whitefield Moor and leads through the scattered outskirts of Brockenhurst village. Continue heading for the village centre, **turn L** over the ford, to ride up the main street. **Turn R** at the Y-junction then **turn R** onto the A337 over the level crossing. (Start the ride here if you arrive by train.)

Continue for 100 yards after the crossing then **turn L** up the lane signed for St Nicholas' parish church. Opposite the church the lane curves right and a peaceful ride brings you to the A337. Cross straight over and continue along the lane ahead to a road. **Turn R** (signed further on for Sway and New Milton). Go under a railway arch and 100 yards further on you come to a bridleway a little on your right leading to the track of the former railway.

This marks the start of a truly wonderful ride with beautiful views over the Forest. **Turn R** to follow the bridleway under an arch and ride over the open Forest, with the low embankment of the former line a short distance away on your right. Shortly the bridleway curves right to join the old railway line by a small, white building, Cater's Cottage. The line bears left. After a cutting the embanked track runs through open forest. Over to your right wide green lawns rise to Hincheslea ridge crowned with splendid trees. You pass Setthorns campsite on your left and 1 mile further on the track ahead is blocked. **Turn L** and follow the path, which curves right to a road. **Turn R** for 150 yards then **turn L**, signed for Burley. At this point the road has been laid over the trackbed of the railway. After a mile you come to Station House, now a tearoom, on your left.

It is a good idea to dismount at this point to make sure you find the

continuation of the trackbed. Walk round Station House, leaving it on your left, and cross the end of the road to Lyndhurst by the cycle sign. Rejoin the trackbed through a small gate half-hidden in the hedge on the other side and enjoy another splendid ride. Cross straight over a minor road past a futuristic building, which replaced the crossing keeper's cottage. The track ends at Burbush car park. Cross the car park and **turn R** for Burley. Pass the village war memorial and the Queen's Head on your left to return to the car park.

• •

BURLEY
Burley was once so remote that it was said to depend for its livelihood on its yearly crop of acorns and beechmast! Not so today. Its narrow main street lined with craft and souvenir shops is a magnet for all who visit the Forest. During the 18th and early 19th century the village thrived on the contraband trade. Smugglers ran luxury goods such as tea and tobacco across the Forest and most of the paths around Burley are smugglers' tracks. The Queen's Head pub was a favourite meeting place.

BROCKENHURST
Like all Forest villages Brockenhurst spreads itself in a comfortable fashion over heaths and around green lawns threaded with streams and shaded by old woods of beech and oak. There must have been a settlement here beside the upper reaches of the Lymington river in Saxon times as the church, alone on a hilltop, has Saxon herringbone masonry in the walls. The church is full of charming features, including a curtained 'Squire's Pew' providing a sleeper with delightful seclusion!

Riding along the embanked track of the former railway near Burley

During the First World War Brockenhurst was the home of a base hospital and if you walk down the east side of the churchyard, you will see the memorial to the New Zealand and Indian soldiers who lie there. Close by is the grave of a local Forest personality, Brusher Mills. You will recognise it by the carved headstone showing Brusher, a handsome bearded gentleman. He lived in a hut in the woods and caught snakes, much valued for their uses in medicine. To find out more about this fascinating character call in at the Snakecatcher Pub.

CASTLEMAN'S CORKSCREW
The railway from Brockenhurst heading west across the Forest through Ringwood and Wimborne was built in 1847. The authorities insisted on a winding route to avoid the wooded areas of the Forest so the railway soon became known as 'Castleman's Corkscrew' after its foremost promoter, Charles Castleman. As Bournemouth expanded, a new line was built in 1888 from Brockenhurst to Christchurch giving a more direct route to Bournemouth and on to Poole and Dorchester. 'Castleman's Corkscrew' became redundant and was closed in the 1960s and 70s. The Station House was originally opened as Christchurch Road station although the town is 7 miles away! As you rejoin the trackbed of the railway opposite Station House, you will see the remains of one of the platforms on the left.

5

The Southern Forest and the Smugglers' Coast

22 miles

This is a ride in two worlds. North of Lymington you ride through enchanting Forest scenery along quiet roads, crossing open heathland and wooded Inclosures. Heading south through New Milton, the scenery changes dramatically as the route brings you to Christchurch Bay and the small village of Barton-on Sea. Barton was one of the villages, perched on clifftops overlooking Christchurch Bay, which during the 18th century thrived on the smuggling trade. At that time there was a heavy duty on luxury goods such as tea, tobacco and spirits and these could be secretly shipped across from France and, with most villagers lending a hand, easily dispersed through the Forest. After cycling through countryside once used by the freetraders you take to the coast at Hordle Cliff and enjoy a magnificent clifftop ride, almost all off-road, to Keyhaven. You return to Lymington along the Ancient Highway. Now a cycleway, this old road runs beside traces of the salterns that once lined the coast from Lymington to Keyhaven.

Maps: OS Landranger 196 The Solent & Isle of Wight and 195 Bournemouth & Purbeck.

Starting point: Lymington car park in St Thomas's Street, behind Marks & Spencer (GR 321953).

By train: Lymington station.

Refreshments: Lymington has a good selection of pubs and tearooms. Several pubs on the route, including the Rising Sun at Wootton and the Gun at Keyhaven. Tearooms and restaurant at the Sammy Miller Museum. Meals and snacks in Barton-on-Sea at the clifftop Beachcomber café.

The route: A generally flat route, 5 miles off-road.

Leave the car park, following the exit sign to a T-junction. **Turn R** to the top of the road. **Turn L**, signed New Milton and Christchurch, and continue to a traffic island. **Turn R** up the road, signed Recreation Centre. At the T-junction by the Musketeer pub turn **R**. After 1¼ miles go straight over the crossroads along Pitmore Lane through pleasant farming country to reach the open Forest at Shirley Holms. The road curves left to a T-junction. **Turn L** along the B3055 for a few yards then **turn R** along Manchester Road

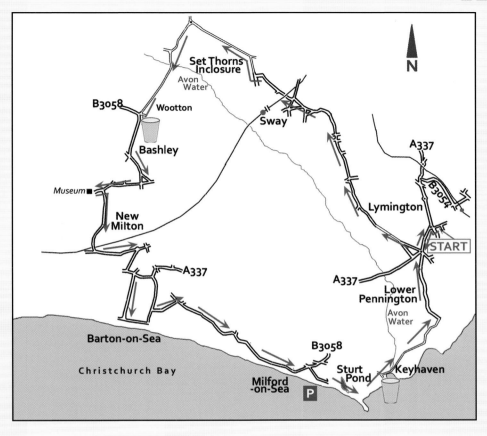

(named after one of the gangs who came here to lay the railway).

Continue under the railway and through the outskirts of Sway village to a T-junction then **turn R** along Brighton Road over the heath to meet a road. **Turn L**, signed Wilverley and Wootton. A beautiful ride close to Set Thorns Inclosure brings you to a T-junction. **Turn L**, signed Burley, Ringwood and Bournemouth, to ride past Wilverley Inclosure. The road dips into a valley. **Turn L**, signed Bashley and Wootton, to cross Wootton Bridge over Avon Water and ride through one of the Forest's loveliest Inclosures. In

front of the Rising Sun pub **turn R** for a few yards then **turn L**, signed New Milton and Bashley.

Ride through Bashley to meet the B3055 at an island. **Turn R** for 1 mile to the Sammy Miller Motorcycle Museum on your left. After your visit **turn R** for 200 yards then **turn R** along Stem Lane. Cross the railway bridge to a T-junction. **Turn L**, signed 'Other Industrial Estates'. After ¾ mile, at the traffic island, **turn R**, signed Lymington and Barton-on-Sea, and continue to a T-junction. **Turn L** along the A337, signed Lymington and Milford-on-Sea, for a short distance to

The magnificent clifftop ride from Hordle Cliff car park

traffic lights. **Turn R**, signed Barton-on-Sea, along Barton Court Road, which brings you to the village. Bear left to the clifftop.

Now you have glorious views over Christchurch Bay. **Turn L** to the end of the clifftop road then **turn L** up Becton Lane for ¼ mile. **Turn R**, signed Milford-on-Sea. The road crosses Becton Bunny, popular with the 18th-century freetraders, and continues to a T-junction. **Turn R**, signed Milford-on-Sea. Pass a car park on the right then, as the road runs down to the coast, **turn R** into the next car park opposite Whitby Road, by a prominent toilet block. (This is Hordle Cliff car park but when I was there the sign was very faint.) Cross the car park to a path tracing the clifftop. **Turn L** to follow the path. This is a great ride with wonderful sea views!

After 1½ miles you come to a gate. **Turn L** to take the path over the grass to the road and **turn R** for 200 yards to the Marine Café. **Turn L** over the café car park and follow the track running beside Sturt Pond, a splendid place for wildlife. Continue beside the Danes Stream, a great favourite with kingfishers.

Turn L over the bridge and keep straight on along the road with the creeks and marshes of Keyhaven Nature Reserve on your right. The road bears left in Keyhaven. With the Gun Inn on your left, **turn R**. Harbour sights and sounds greet you as you cross the sluice gates over Avon Water. Gulls screech overhead and busy little turnstones scamper along the water's edge, tipping the pebbles over in their search for food. Pass a car park on your right and keep straight on along the Ancient

Lymington Harbour

Highway signed 'Cycle Path to Lymington'. Go through a gate and follow the lane heading north through Lower Pennington to a T-junction. **Turn L** to the traffic island then **turn R** for Lymington town centre. **Turn R** at the junction, signed New Milton, then **turn L** into St Thomas's Street. **Turn R** into the car park just past Marks & Spencer.

● ●

THE SAMMY MILLER MUSEUM

A visit to this splendid museum, which is claimed to house the finest collection of fully restored motorcycles in Europe, can be enjoyed by everyone. Apart from the bikes there are memorabilia spanning seven decades of motorcycling for sport and pleasure. The buildings are grouped around an attractive courtyard where you might be tempted to enjoy the animals and birds before seeing the bikes! Sammy Miller has devoted his life to motorcycle racing and has been eleven times successive British Champion and twice European Champion. In 2009 he was awarded the MBE in recognition of his services to the sport. The museum is open every day from 10 am to 4.30 pm. The tearoom and restaurant are open from 9 am to 4.30 pm at weekends and from 10 am to 4.30 pm during the week. Telephone: 01425 620777/616644.

Abbey Lands

16 miles

This magical ride west of the Beaulieu River is one of my favourite tours. Leaving Beaulieu you enter a different world as you follow tranquil grass-bordered lanes through remote countryside once farmed by the monks from Beaulieu Abbey. This delightful landscape of scattered farms and small villages set among fields and copses still bears their imprint and is very different from the Crown lands of the open Forest. There is much to discover, including a path to the sea giving splendid views over the Solent to the Isle of Wight and finally a Forest treasure, Buckler's Hard, a perfectly preserved 18th-century village. On its slipways sturdy Forest oaks were used to build some of the ships for Nelson's navy.

Map: OS Landranger 196 The Solent & Isle of Wight.

Starting point: Beaulieu village car park. The best approach is via the A326, the Fawley road. Turn off, following the sign for Beaulieu, along the B3054. From the A35 heading east from Lyndhurst, turn right for Beaulieu along the B3056. The car park is signed off the road that runs beside the pond (GR 386022).

By train: Beaulieu Road station is 2 miles away but it is a pleasant Forest ride.

Refreshments: Tearooms in Beaulieu and Buckler's Hard. The Master Builder's House Hotel has a welcoming Yachtsman's Bar.

The route: An easy route along quiet country lanes, off-road for the last 2 miles.

From Beaulieu car park take the path leading past tearooms to Beaulieu High Street. **Turn R** up the street to the main road. **Turn L**, signed Lymington and Brockenhurst, then shortly after **turn L** again, following the brown sign for Buckler's Hard. You pass Beufre Farm on your right, named after the oxen used by the monks to pull their heavy ploughs.

At the T-junction **turn R**, signed East Boldre. The lane curves left past the evocatively-named Grindstone Cottages. Continue along Lodge Lane with its beautfully wooded grass verges for 1½ miles. The lane curves right past Lodge Farm then shortly left to bring you to a T-junction by Thorns Corner Cottages. **Turn R**, signed East End, along St Leonards Road. Continue for 1¼ miles to meet a road. **Turn L**,

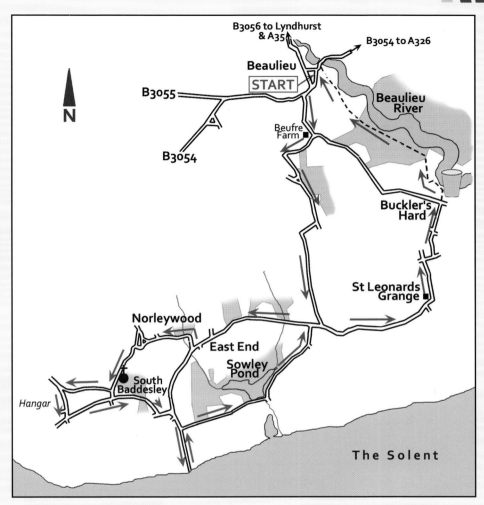

signed Lymington and Norleywood. As you ride past some of the outlying houses of East End there is a finger of open Forest land on your right, forming an interesting contrast with the rest of this tour.

At the next T-junction **turn R**, signed Boldre and Norleywood. The road curves left to Norleywood. Keep straight on past the turnings into the village on your right to cross the bridge by the ford over Plummers Water. In ½ mile you will see South Baddesley church on your left. This homely little church, described by Pevsner as 'rustic and jolly', is well worth a visit. At the next junction **turn R**. Now for some tricky navigation! Continue for ½ mile then **turn sharp L** along an unmarked lane. Shortly, on your right, a large blister hangar marks the site of Lymington's wartime airfield. Just past the hangar there is an information

33

Looking over the Solent from Tanners Lane

plaque on the corner of the Solent Way track.

At the crossroads **turn L** along the lane skirting Pylewell Park, a private estate, on your right. The lane swings left to a T-junction. **Turn R**, signed Sowley and Buckler's Hard. After 200 yards at the Y-junction turn right down Tanners Lane, which runs down to an idyllic shingle beach, with a magnificent view of the Isle of Wight from the Needles in the west to Cowes in the east. This is an ideal spot for a picnic among the trees fringing the shore.

Return up Tanners Lane and **turn R**, signed Sowley and Buckler's Hard. After 1 mile you will see Sowley Pond on your left. The monks required a great deal of fish and dammed several small streams to create the pond. Today woods shade its shores and it is a haven for wildlife, but in the 17th and 18th centuries there was an ironworks here. The water-powered tilt-hammers worked the ironstone brought from Hengistbury Head and the beaches at Hordle.

Continue along the lane to a T-junction. **Turn R**, signed Buckler's Hard and St Leonards. The monks used much of their land for grazing their sheep and on your left you pass Bergerie, French for a sheep-farm, which recalls those days. Another reminder is the ruins at St Leonards,

Buckler's Hard village

which you pass a little later. St Leonards was a grange for the lay brothers who worked the fields. Close to the road is the east end of a huge barn once used to store the produce, with a modern barn built within its confines. Over the wall, across the field close to Grange House, are the ruins of the lay brothers' chapel, still preserving a little delicate tracery within a window arch.

At the next junction, take the first **turn R** signed Buckler's Hard. This brings you to a lane crossing the top of the grassy lawns above Buckler's Hard village. Gaining access to the village on a bike is not easy as there are no signs until you actually get there! **Turn L** along the road signed Beaulieu for a few yards, then **turn R** down the drive leading to the Master Builder's House Hotel. Just before the cattle grid, **turn R** to go through a gate with a notice 'Cyclists Please Dismount' and **turn L** to wheel your bike between the wide lawns fronting the rows of cottages down to the Beaulieu river.

Turn L to ride the riverside path, signed Solent Way, for 2 miles, which brings you back to Beaulieu village by the Montagu Arms Hotel. **Turn L** to the car park entrance by the sports car showrooms.

LYMINGTON AIRFIELD
The airfield was constructed by the RAF in 1943 as a model for the type of Advanced Landing Grounds that would need to be built in France after the Allies

35

landed on D-Day. The airfield became operational in April 1944 with the arrival of the 50th Fighter Group from America who flew their P-47 Thunderbolt aircraft in missions over France during and after D-Day. The Group moved to France at the end of June and the airfield was not used again.

BUCKLER'S HARD

Today this small village is a quiet place, perfect in Ratty's words for 'messing about in boats', enjoying a picnic or watching the abundant wildlife. But once the village would have been alive with noise and bustle. Down on the slipways you would have heard the shouts of workmen, the rasp of saws and the thud of hammers as the planks of great warships were shaped and fastened into place. If you buy a ticket, you can visit the fascinating museum and visit historic cottages and the tiny chapel.

A plaque and blister hangar mark the site of Lymington's wartime airfield

7
The Solent Shore
16 miles

I f you like the sea and ships, this is the ride for you! Starting from the picturesque New Forest village of Beaulieu, a quiet moorland road leads you south to the sea, with glorious views over the Solent to the Isle of Wight hills. Heading north the route takes you to Ashlett Creek, a tiny haven for small boats beside Southampton Water. On the way you can stop to explore Exbury's world-famous gardens, enjoy a trip on a steam railway, and stroll along the beach in Lepe Country Park to discover relics of the wartime dock where parts of the Mulberry Harbour were constructed.

Map: OS Landranger 196 The Solent & Isle of Wight.

Starting point: Beaulieu village car park. The best approach is via the A326, the Fawley road. Turn off, following the sign for Beaulieu, along the B3054. From the A35 heading east from Lyndhurst turn right for Beaulieu along the B3056. The car park is signed off the road that runs beside the pond (GR 386022).

By train: Beaulieu Road station is 2 miles away but it is a pleasant Forest ride.

Refreshments: Tearooms in Beaulieu, full meals and snacks at Exbury Gardens, café at Lepe Country Park. Pubs: the Royal Oak at Hill Top, the Jolly Sailor at Ashlett Creek, the Falcon in Fawley, the Bridge Tavern at Ipers Bridge.

The route: An easy, mostly flat route along Forest roads and quiet country lanes.

A great abbey was founded by Cistercian monks at Beaulieu in 1204. Now only ruins remain but, as you begin this ride, you have a wonderful view over the wide stretch of water that was formerly the monks' fishpond. **Turn R** from the car park exit. The fishpond is on your left. Cross the foot of Beaulieu village street then bear left, leaving the Montagu Arms Hotel on your right. The road curves right beside the Beaulieu river. Green lawns slope

down to the riverside – a perfect place to picnic and feed the ducks. The grey stone walls of the abbey precinct are on your left and, as you ride beside the river, you will catch glimpses of some of the ruins, including Palace House, which was built around the former abbey gatehouse.

The road runs up to a junction at Hill Top. On your right you will see the Royal Oak pub. **Turn R**, signed Eling

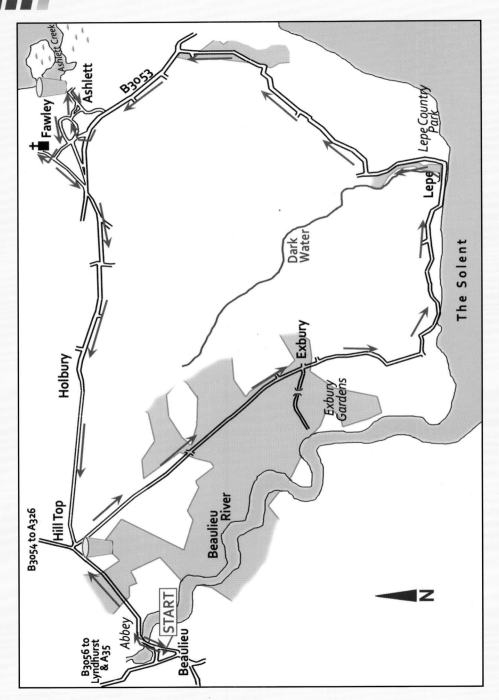

By the Beaulieu river

and Holbury, then almost immediately **turn R** again, signed Lepe and Exbury. Follow this pleasant road through the Forest for 3 miles to Exbury. On your right is the entrance to Exbury Gardens.

Cross the top of Exbury village street and keep straight ahead along Inchmery Lane to catch your first view of the Solent. The road curves left to follow the Solent shore to a T-junction. **Turn R**, signed Lepe, and keep ahead past a row of coastguard cottages and a white watchtower to reach the waterside at Lepe Country Park. This delightful park with its extensive views from Hurst Castle to Portsmouth's Spinnaker Tower has something for everybody and is well worth a visit.

Follow the road as it curves left, signed Blackfield and Langley, to leave the park on your right. Now for some tricky navigation! After only ¼ mile, opposite some cottages, **turn sharp R** along Stanswood Road (it is signed Calshot but you can't see the sign until you are round the corner). An attractive lane winds its way over the Dark Water stream to bring you to the B3053. **Turn L**, signed Fawley, for 1½ miles then **turn R**, signed Fawley, with a sign for the Jolly Sailor pub on the left. Ride into Fawley village and **turn R** along Ashlett Road (2nd turning on the right). The road runs downhill to the creek, a lovely place with a wide green where you can sit and watch small boats bobbing at anchor and beyond them all the ceaseless activity of Southampton Water.

Turn L to retrace your route uphill, passing the Jolly Sailor pub on your right. **Turn R** along the next road on

The steam railway at Exbury tours the world-famous gardens

the right, Copthorne Lane. At the T-junction **turn L**. This brings you quickly to another T-junction. **Turn R** along Church Lane to yet another T-junction. **Turn R** along Marsh Lane to the church, which dates back to Norman times and has a beautifully-carved arch over the west door.

Turn L from the church and keep ahead along Marsh Lane to meet the B3053. **Turn R** for a few yards then **turn L**, signed Beaulieu. After ¼ mile **turn R**, signed Beaulieu. Follow the Beaulieu signs, crossing straight over the road at the traffic lights. A peaceful moorland road over Ipers Bridge brings you back to Hill Top. **Turn L** for

Beaulieu village to return to the car park.

● ●

BEAULIEU

The Saxon name beo-ley, meaning the bee meadow, proved too much for the Norman scribes compiling the Domesday Book and they settled for beau lieu, the beautiful place. And this riverside village could have no better name! Attractive houses line its narrow-paved street but Beaulieu's glory is the remains of its former abbey. The ruined cloisters are still beautiful and some buildings remain, including the monks' refectory, which is now the parish church. Palace House, the home of the Montagu family since 1538, is now open for visitors and you are shown round by costumed guides who recall the workings of the great house in Victorian times. In the grounds is the National Motor Museum, a priceless collection of 250 classic, vintage cars, modern rally cars, the latest F1 machines, and world land speed record breakers including Campbell's famous *Bluebird*. There are picnic areas, cafés and bars. Open every day (except Christmas Day); October to May 10 am to 5 pm, end of May to end of September 10 am to 6 pm. Telephone: 01590 612345 or 01590 612123.

EXBURY GARDENS

These magnificent gardens beside the Beaulieu river contain the Rothschild collection of rhododendrons, azaleas and camellias, as well as rare trees and shrubs. A trip on the miniature steam railway around the gardens is a must! Open March to November, 10 am to 5 pm. Telephone the information line: 02380 899422.

LEPE COUNTRY PARK

Apart from the park's stunning views, there is a great deal to do, especially for children, including nature trails and an adventure playground. You can picnic, swim in the sea and fly kites on the clifftop. Surrounded by nature reserves, the park teems with wildlife. Call in at the office by the café and shop for more information. The park is open every day from 7.30 am to dusk. Telephone: 02380 899108.

Ashlett Creek

A New Forest Safari

17 miles

Although Longleat has no need to fear competition from the New Forest, animals are one of the Forest's greatest attractions, particularly the ponies with their charming leggy foals. All the family, especially children, will enjoy this short tour, which tells some of the ponies' centuries-old story. Their grazing has helped to shape the Forest we know today and they play an important part in the Forest's economy. They are semi-wild, with uncertain tempers, so it is wise not to feed them, however pleading they look! Although they are free to roam, they all have owners and are properly cared for. They belong to the Commoners, people living in or close to the Forest who possess rights dating from Saxon times, attached to their land. The most important was the right to pasture not only ponies but also cattle, donkeys and, in autumn, pigs, in the Forest. All the animals are convinced they have right-of-way on the roads so it is wise to give them a wide berth!

The tour starts in Ashurst, a pleasantly leafy village on the eastern border of the Forest. After Lyndhurst, quiet roads lead you through the Forest to Beaulieu Road station. Opposite the station is the site of the Beaulieu Road pony sales. The road dips into the Beaulieu river valley and you have an opportunity to visit Beaulieu with its famous Motor Museum, Palace House, the home of the Montagu family, and historic abbey ruins. On the return run find time if you can to visit the New Forest Wildlife Park, where animals from further afield roam free in their natural surroundings, and Longdown Activity Farm which is also on the route.

Map: OS Landranger 196 The Solent & Isle of Wight.

Starting point: Ashurst public car park. Turn off the A35 for the shops, following the parking sign, pass the Happy Cheese pub on your left and cross the road leading to the hospital to the car park on your left (GR 335103).

By train: Ashurst (New Forest) station.

Refreshments: Restaurants and cafés in Ashurst, refreshments at the Wildlife Park and the Activity Farm. Pubs at Ashurst, Beaulieu Road and Arters Lawn.

The route: Easy, no hills.

Turn R from the entrance to Ashurst car park, cross the road leading to the hospital and turn left over the railway bridge, following signs for Lyndhurst.

Follow the cycle path to the right of the A35. Continue towards Lyndhurst and **turn L**, signed Beaulieu, along the first road on the left, the B3056.

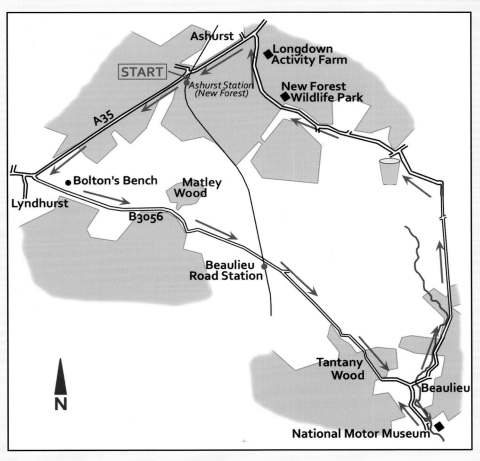

On either side are open lawns cropped short by the ponies. The dome-shaped hill crowned with trees on your left is called Bolton's Bench, named after Lord Bolton who was Lord Warden of the Forest in 1688.

Continue over the heath, following the signs for Beaulieu. On your left you have magnificent views east over the heath to distant woodland. Trees crowd close to the road as you pass the campsite at Matley Wood, one of the most beautiful oak woods in the Forest. It is home to deer, badgers and foxes

and a very rare bird, the lesser spotted woodpecker. Matley is a perfect place for a ramble.

The road runs over open heath to Beaulieu Road station. You may wonder as you see just a handful of cottages, a pub and a hotel, why such a lonely place should merit a stop on the main line! Opened by the Southampton & Dorchester Railway in 1847, the company was obliged to install it as a 'personal' station for Lord Montagu for allowing the railway to be built over part of his estate. A special signal told

Emerging from the Forest into bright sunshine (photo by Dick Snell)

train drivers when they had to stop for Lord Montagu and his guests. The fenced pens opposite the station come to life during the pony sales held several times a year.

Continue heading for Beaulieu past Pig Bush and Tantany Wood, reminders of the days when the Cistercian monks at the abbey farmed these lands. They evidently pastured pigs on the acorns and beechmast in Tantany Wood as it is named after St Anthony, the patron saint of pigs! The entrance to all the Beaulieu attractions is on your left as you approach the village.

Retrace your route from Beaulieu for ¾ mile then **turn R**, signed Ipley Cross. The lane goes over the Beaulieu river, which is just a stream at this point. Go straight over the crossroads, signed Colbury. Continue round a sharp left bend to a junction just after the Bold Forester pub and **turn L**, signed Colbury, along Arters Lawn. After 1¼ miles you come to the entrance to the New Forest Wildlife Park on your right. After your visit **turn R** from the entrance and continue along the lane to Longdown Activity Farm, also on your right. If you have children with you, by the time they have fed all the baby animals at the farm it is time to head for home! So **turn R** from the entrance to the farm to continue to the A35 and **turn L** to return to Ashurst.

BEAULIEU ROAD PONY SALES
During the summer when the foals are well grown you may see the Commoners

on horseback galloping across the Forest trying to round up as many ponies as they can in a certain area. Once the ponies are in the pound, the Agisters, who are responsible for over-seeing all aspects of the ponies on the Forest, clip the tails of the young colts in various ways as proof that the appropriate fees have been paid. The Commoners can claim the foals that run with their particular mares. In autumn colt hunting begins for the sales at Beaulieu Road. New Forest ponies are strong, naturally swift and sure-footed. They are fast for their size, extremely hardy and, once you have gained their affection and trust, good-tempered. If you are inclined to buy one, you may find it an investment as New Forest ponies are splendid jumpers! For times of the sales consult the website www.new-forest-national-park.com/beaulieu-road-pony-sales or look in the local papers.

THE NEW FOREST WILDLIFE PARK

This delightful wildlife park covers 25 acres of ancient woodland and a wander round the park reveals a wonderful range of animals, including otters, wolves, polecats, pine martens, lynx and wild boar. Watch tiny harvest mice making their homes on top of corn stalks and visit the night barn to see badgers curled up asleep in their underground setts. You can even adopt one of the animals if you wish! And for delicious teas and light refreshments I recommend the Woodland Bakehouse Tearoom – one of my favourite places! Open all the year; summer 10 am to 5.30 pm, winter 10 am to dusk. Telephone: 02380 292408.

The entrance to the New Forest Wildlife Park

Ponies passing the time of day by the roadside

LONGDOWN ACTIVITY FARM

The farm provides fun for all the family as everyone can join in the daily schedule of activities. Among the many friendly animals is their gentle giant, Billy the Shire horse. If it rains, indoor play areas include trampolines, a ball pool and the straw bale barn. There is a tearoom, gift shop and picnic areas. Open daily from mid February to the end of October 10 am to 5 pm, also weekends in November and December and daily just before Christmas. Telephone: 02380 292857.

Hampshire Backwaters

17 miles

This tour in less well-known countryside west of Romsey is one of my favourite rides. I find it just as rewarding in its quiet way as the more popular areas. The route runs through a well-wooded landscape threaded with streams, following the river valleys of the Test and the Dun. The small town of Romsey, clustered around its ancient abbey, makes the perfect starting point. From Romsey you head north, following the valley of the Test. A streamside ride through woods leads you west past two beautiful hamlets before you head north again to the Dun valley. You follow the Dun to Butt's Green near Lockerley then turn south along undulating lanes giving wonderful views over the Test valley. The lanes descend into the valley of the Blackwater to bring you to one of Hampshire's most honoured places, the grave of Florence Nightingale in St Margaret's churchyard at East Wellow. At the request of her relatives she was buried close to her childhood home, Embley Park. You will glimpse the house across the meadows as you head east to return to Romsey.

Map: OS Landranger 185 Winchester & Basingstoke.

Starting point: Alma long-stay car park, off Alma Road, Romsey (GR 356213).

By train: Romsey station.

Refreshments: Good pubs and restaurants in Romsey. There are pubs along the Test valley and at Dunbridge and Butt's Green. Tearooms at the World of Water, at the caravan site in Mount Lane, Bramley's, Gilberts' Garden Centre and Dandy's Ford Fisheries.

The route: Most of the route is easy but there is a hilly 2-mile section between Butt's Green and Dandy's Ford.

Turn **L** from the exit of Alma car park to head north along Alma Road. Keep straight ahead at the lights, following the sign for Stockbridge, along the A3057. At the T-junction **turn R**, signed Stockbridge, and at the next junction follow the road round to the right to go under the railway. Continue up the valley. On your right you pass the World of Water, which has a separate, very good café. The road crosses the Test. Shortly after **turn L**, signed Lockerley, Dunbridge and Awbridge along the B3084.

At the next junction follow the B3084 bearing right, signed Lockerley, Dunbridge and Awbridge. Now be ready for some careful navigation! Pass the turning for Stanbridge Earls School

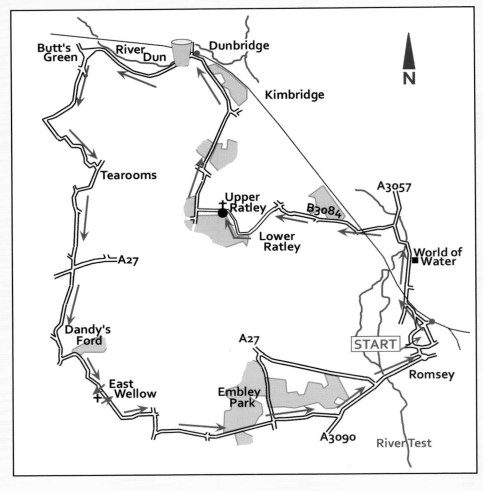

on your left and a lane on your right. Continue for 300 yards then leave the B3084 and **turn L** along Coombe Lane (unsigned but there is a sign for a Single Track Road). The lane winds through woods surrounding small lakes and streams past the thatched houses of Lower and Upper Ratley. Pass the church on your left to a T-junction. **Turn R** out of Church Lane and keep on for ½ mile to a T-junction by a war memorial. **Turn L**, signed Kimbridge and Lockerley, then immediately

turn R, signed Dunbridge and Kimbridge.

The road runs to meet the B3084. **Turn L**, signed Broughton, Mottisfont and Dunbridge. Opposite Dunbridge station the B3084 turns sharply right. Leave the B3084 at this point, keeping straight on, signed Lockerley, passing a pub on your left. A pleasant lane leads ahead through the meadows with the River Dun on your right. After 1 mile the lane runs close to the riverside and

A bridge over the River Dun

a footpath leads a few yards to a bridge over the river. This makes a lovely spot to take a break!

Pass the green at Butt's Green to a crossroads and **turn L**, signed Romsey. After 300 yards you come to a junction of several lanes. **Turn R** into Cooks Lane then immediately **turn L** into Mount Lane. You pass a caravan site on your left, which has tearooms. The lane continues winding south for a mile to a T-junction. **Turn R**, passing Bramley's tearooms on your left, and at the next junction follow the road round to the left.

Cross straight over the A27 to follow Dandy's Ford Lane. There are tearooms at the garden centre on the right and yet more tearooms at Dandy's Ford

Fishery a little further on, also on your right. Pass a lane on your right and shortly look for a sign for Wellow church on your right, indicating a lane on your left. **Turn L** for Wellow church and in ½ mile turn right to the church. Florence Nightingale's grave is marked by a white four-sided monument with inscriptions on each side for four family members. Florence's inscription bears only 'F.N. 1820–1910', in accordance with her wishes.

After your visit to St Margaret's, return to the lane and **turn R** to a T-junction. **Turn R** then after a few yards **turn L**, signed Romsey. Pass the lane to the golf club and look left to see Embley Park, now a school, across the fields. After ½ mile you come to a T-junction. **Turn L** then immediately **turn R**, signed

Medieval wall paintings depict the life of St Margaret in East Wellow church

Romsey, to meet the A3090. **Turn L** to swoop downhill, cross the Test, and follow the signs to Alma long-stay car park.

● ●

ROMSEY

Romsey's splendid abbey has been described as 'music in stone'. Dating from the early 12th century it was built on the site of an earlier Saxon church and the foundations can still be seen beneath a trapdoor. Most impressive is the Norman nave, which rises to a height of 70 ft. Among many of the abbey's treasures are 14th-century tiles, an Anglo-Saxon rood and some exquisite modern tapestries. Today, many people visit the abbey to pay their last respects to Lord Louis, Earl Mountbatten of Burma, who lived at Broadlands nearby and is buried close to his family pew. Romsey's oldest house, King John's House, was built in

1240 for a merchant. It is now a museum. The garden has been laid out to reflect the property's age. The house is open from Spring Bank Holiday to the end of September, 10 am to 4 pm, Monday to Saturday.

ST MARGARET'S CHURCH, EAST WELLOW

This homely little church is charming. The heavily-timbered roof of the 13th-century nave and chancel is supported by five massive wooden pillars and the walls retain some of their medieval wall paintings. Resting in one of the windowsills is a replica of the Scutari Cross made of bullets from the Crimea (the original was stolen). Beside it are photographs of Florence Nightingale and a framed text that was hanging in her bedroom in the house in Park Lane where she died.

Away From It All – North of Romsey

20 miles

As the Test flows lazily south towards Romsey the landscape east of the river changes. Rolling downland gives way to low hills, broad fertile meadows and copse woods. Narrow grass-bordered lanes lead to small villages and hamlets so remote and peaceful you feel they can have no connection with our 21st century! The tour starts in Horsebridge, a tiny village perched on the east bank of the Test, 3 miles south of Stockbridge. You cross the Test and head south to Mottisfont, famous for its priory and gardens bordering the river. Then you turn east to explore this very different countryside before the route climbs the downs to Farley Mount Country Park. The park is a Site of Special Scientific Interest covering 1,000 acres of woods and downland, with wonderful views, just perfect for walks and picnics. Heading west you return through the attractive village of King's Somborne then descend the final mile to the car park in Horsebridge.

Map: OS Landranger 185 Winchester & Basingstoke.

Starting point: Horsebridge car park near King's Somborne. Heading south, follow the A3057 from Stockbridge for 3 miles to King's Somborne. Continue south from the village for ¾ mile, then turn right for Horsebridge. Turn right in the village to a track on the left opposite the former John of Gaunt Inn, which leads to the car park (GR 345303).

By train: Mottisfont & Dunbridge station; start the route in Mottisfont (1½ miles distant).

Refreshments: Pubs in King's Somborne and Braishfield. Tearooms at Mottisfont.

The route: An easy route with no steep climbs.

Before leaving the car park, follow the footpath on the right, the Test Way, for a few yards to catch a glimpse of Horsebridge station, beautifully preserved with signal box and platforms intact.

To start the ride, **turn L** from the car park entrance to leave the John of Gaunt Inn (now sadly closed) on your right and cross a bridge over one of the streams of the Test. John of Gaunt, fourth son of Edward III, held the manor here in the 14th century. The

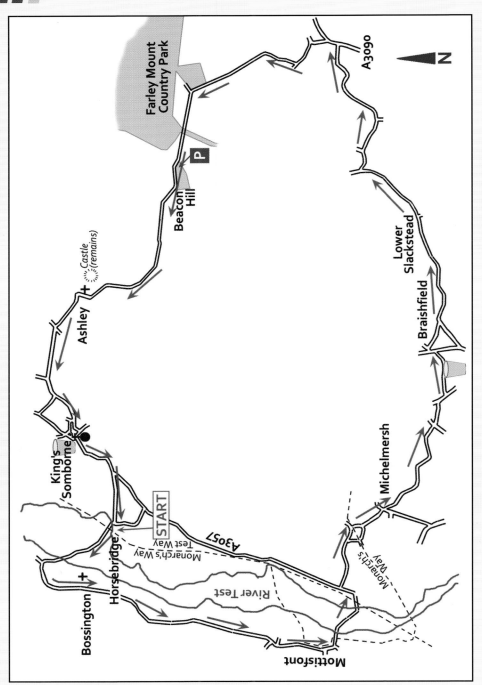

Horsebridge station

road passes the watermill at Houghton and at the Y-junction curves round to the left, signed Dunbridge, Broughton and Nether Wallop. Keep ahead at the next junction, signed Mottisfont and Pittleworth. On your left you will see Bossington Park. It was once the site of a village but now only the church remains.

As you head south the road runs fairly high to give views over the river valley. After 3 miles keep straight on, past the main gates of Mottisfont Priory, following the sign for Michelmersh and Timsbury along Mottisfont Lane. The lane curves left to the visitor entrance on your left. After a visit, **turn L** from the entrance to resume the tour. The road crosses the Test, with a glorious view of the river to a T-junction with the A3057. **Turn L**, signed Stockbridge

and King's Somborne, for 300 yards. Careful navigation needed now! **Turn R** along the first road on the right (unsigned). The road runs for 1 mile into Michelmersh village. **Turn R** at the T-junction and continue for 300 yards then at the Y-junction **turn L**, signed Braishfield. Keep straight on over the crossroads, signed Braishfield.

The road curves left past Hunts Farm to bring you to a staggered crossroads. Although the sign indicates a left turn for Braishfield **keep straight on** down the unsigned road to a T-junction. **Turn R** for a few yards then **turn L** for Braishfield into Newport Lane. Pass the pub to a T-junction. **Turn L** for just a few yards then **turn R**, signed Winchester and Slackstead. Continue for only 50 yards to a Y-junction. Bear right through this very attractive

Ashley's Norman church is built within the earthworks of a former castle

village, past the pond to a junction. Bear left for Lower Slackstead. Keep ahead for Hursley and Winchester to a Y-junction. **Turn R**, signed Winchester and Hursley.

The road climbs through woods then runs downhill to meet the A3090. **Turn L**, signed Winchester, for 200 yards then **turn L**, signed Farley Mount and Sparsholt. After 300 yards you come to a T-junction. **Turn L** along the unsigned road (the right turn is signed Sparsholt). This is Farley Mount Road, which climbs steadily for a mile to meet the road running along the foot of the Mount. **Turn L** along the road.

There are splendid opportunities for walks from all the parking areas but if

you only have time for a short walk I recommend you continue west for ¾ mile to a car park on the left and have a look at the famous horse monument – see 'Beacon Hill' overleaf.

From the car park, the road swings right to head north to Ashley. The church and part of the village stand in the outer bailey of a Norman castle built around AD 1200. The church of St Mary is a rare survival of a Norman church of that date with very few later additions. There is just a simple nave and chancel with a tiny round-headed entrance. South of the churchyard you can see part of the castle's remaining earthworks.

The road bears left for King's Somborne

to a T-junction. **Turn L**, signed King's Somborne. At the next T-junction **turn R** along Church Road. Pass the church on your left and continue to meet the A3057. **Turn L** and continue for ½ mile then **turn R** for Horsebridge. **Turn R**, signed Houghton, and **turn L** opposite the former John of Gaunt Inn to return to your car.

HORSEBRIDGE STATION

The station is privately owned today but once it was one of the stops on the London & South Western Railway running between Andover and Redbridge near Southampton. It was known as the 'Sprat and Winkle' line because it carried seafood inland from the south coast.

MOTTISFONT

This charming village of mellow brick and thatch dates back to Saxon times. The name is derived from the Saxon word for a meeting place, a moot, which was beside a spring or font. The spring still rises to form a deep pool in the grounds of Mottisfont Priory, now the property of the National Trust. The present mansion incorporates part of a 13th-century Augustinian priory. The beautiful grounds are crossed by a branch of the Test, which flows serenely through lawns shaded by ancient trees, but pride of place must go to the gorgeous collection of old-fashioned roses in the former walled kitchen garden. The gardens, shop, café and house are open every day from 10 am to 5 pm from mid February to the end of October. For other times, telephone: 01794 340757.

BEACON HILL

From the Beacon Hill car park in Farley Mount Country Park, a short walk west along a footpath will take you to one of the park's strangest features, a pyramid-shaped monument built on top of an Iron Age burial mound. This marks the grave of a horse that saved the life of its owner, Paulet St John, in 1733, by carrying him safely over a chalk pit 25 ft deep.

The Test Valley and the Wallop Brook

22 miles

Following grass-bordered lanes along two beautiful but very different river valleys, combined with a thrilling ride over sweeping downland, makes this tour north of Romsey a favourite of mine. Starting from the old market town of Stockbridge you cross the Test to cycle beside the river, which meanders through broad meadows framed by wooded hillsides. The route rises to take you high on the downs then plunges into the steep-sided valley of the Wallop Brook, which flows swiftly through several picturesque villages lined with many deep-thatched, half-timbered houses. On the way you can step back into the Iron Age with a visit to Danebury Ring – a magnificent hill fort – then be brought back to the present day by calling in at the Museum of Army Flying near Middle Wallop. Allow plenty of time for this tour – there are many tempting refreshment stops along the way.

Map: OS Landranger 185 Winchester & Basingstoke.

Starting point: The main street (A30) in Stockbridge, heading west from GR 359351. There is ample roadside parking.

By train: No convenient train.

Refreshments: Stockbridge has excellent restaurants and cafés and there are pubs in all the villages. The Museum of Army Flying has a licensed restaurant.

The route: No busy roads. Undulating, but not strenuous.

From the parking area beside the main street in Stockbridge, head west to cross the River Test. Immediately **turn R**, signed Longstock. There is also a brown sign for Longstock Park Gardens. Straight away you are out in the countryside with beautiful views over the river on your right. Continue through Longstock. Pass the pub and after ¾ mile **turn R**, signed Fullerton and Wherwell.

You pass the entrance to Longstock Park Gardens on your left and, still following the Test, you ride through the park. Pass Fullerton Grange on your left. At this point the River Anton flows into the Test and you leave the river valley to climb the downs. At the Y-junction **turn L**, signed Red Rice.

Go straight over a crossroads and continue over the downs for 2 miles to a lane on the left. **Turn L**, signed Red

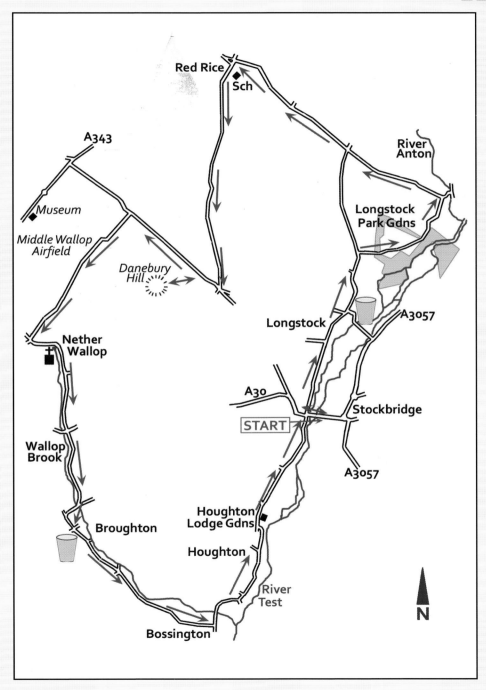

Red Rice
Sch

A343

Museum

Middle Wallop
Airfield

Danebury
Hill

River
Anton

Longstock
Park Gdns

A3057

Longstock

Nether
Wallop

A30

START

Stockbridge

A3057

Wallop
Brook

Houghton
Lodge Gdns

Broughton

Houghton

River
Test

Bossington

N

Longstock, one of the attractive villages seen on this tour

Rice, past Farley School on your left. Head south for 2¼ miles then **turn sharp R**, signed The Wallops. On your left Danebury Hill, crowned with its ring of beech trees, dominates the landscape. If you leave your bike in the parking area, you can walk up to this splendid fort.

Turn L from the entrance to the car park to resume the route of the tour and be ready for some tricky navigation. After 1¼ miles you come to a narrow unsigned lane on your left (it's the first lane on the left). **Turn L** to continue the tour. If you wish to visit the Museum of Army Flying, do not turn left but keep straight on for 1 mile to the A343. **Turn L** for ¾ mile to the museum. After your visit return to the unsigned lane and **turn R** to continue the tour.

The lane leaves the downs to pass Middle Wallop airfield on your right and drops rather suddenly to a T-junction in Nether Wallop village. **Turn L** into Farley Street with the Wallop Brook flowing under bridges on your right. You might like to pause and explore this attractive village. The church, which dates back to Saxon times and retains some medieval wall paintings, stands on a hill with extensive views over the valley.

Follow the road beside the Wallop Brook, signed Broughton. Go straight over a crossroads, still following the sign for Broughton. As you enter Broughton follow the road signed Romsey to cross the brook. Keep to the same road as it curves left in the village, signed Houghton, Tytherley and Romsey. At the T-junction opposite the Greyhound pub **turn L** to ride through the village. Keep ahead for 2 miles to a T-junction at Bossington. **Turn L.** On your right the Wallop Brook flows into the Test, and you are now riding north along the Test valley. The road curves right to a Y-junction. **Turn L**, signed Stockbridge and Houghton.

Continue through Houghton. After 1 mile you will see the entrance to Houghton Lodge and Gardens on your right. At the T-junction you meet the outbound route. **Turn R** to cross the Test into Stockbridge.

● ●

LONGSTOCK PARK GARDENS

The water gardens are open on the first and third Sunday of the month from April to September, 2 pm to 5 pm. Telephone: 01264 810904.

DANEBURY HILL FORT

The massive ramparts of the fort enclose a living area of 12 acres, home for a farming community during the Iron Age, which lasted from around 800 BC to the coming of the Romans in AD 43. Society was well organised. The houses were mostly circular, 20–30 ft across with thatched roofs and wattle and daub walls. Produce from neighbouring farmsteads was stored in huts and pits. The people worked leather and wood, as well as metal, and loom weights indicate spinning and weaving. Religion was important and a temple or shrines crowned the highest point inside the fort. Sling stones were used for defence but warriors would first ride into battle with

Danebury Iron Age hill fort

spears and shields. The site has been extensively excavated by Prof Barry Cunliffe whose book *Danebury: Anatomy of an Iron Age Hill Fort* is published by Batsford.

ARMY AIR CORPS MIDDLE WALLOP

During the Second World War the new Middle Wallop airfield was occupied by the RAF, and was one of the front-line fighter stations. Spitfires, Hurricanes, Beaufighters and Blenheims were mainly used and some dispersal points of the old grass airfield are still there. In 1957, when British Army aviation became independent of the RAF, Middle Wallop transferred to the new Army Air Corps. It became the School of Army Aviation, the base where most Army Air Corps pilots begin their careers.

MUSEUM OF ARMY FLYING

This fascinating museum with its many historic aircraft tells the story of Army Flying from the days of Sam Cody to the present. There are simulators, a rifle range and an exciting children's corner. The 1940s house is a grim reminder of daily life during the war years.
Open daily, 10 am to 4.30 pm.
Telephone: 01264 784421.

HOUGHTON LODGE AND GARDENS

Glorious gardens, with lawns reaching down to the River Test. Open every day except Wednesday from 1st March to 31st October, 10 am to 5 pm.
Telephone: 01264 810502.

The Test winds through the meadows near Stockbridge

12

In the Hampshire Highlands

22 miles

This exciting tour is set in the hills of north-west Hampshire, a beautiful area often called the 'Hampshire Highlands'. Although not quite alpine there are several challenging climbs in the remote middle section of the route but you are rewarded with wonderful views, and an exhilarating 6-mile descent. The tour finishes with a gentle meander along the charming Bourne valley. It starts in Hurstbourne Tarrant, one of Hampshire's most attractive villages and a great favourite with Jane Austen. You will discover more old-world villages tucked in the folds of the hills. Among them is the tiny hamlet of Crux Easton where you will find a rare, fully restored, 19th-century wind engine.

Maps: OS Landranger 185 Winchester & Basingstoke and 174 Newbury & Wantage.

Starting point: Hurstbourne Tarrant parish car park. Hurstbourne Tarrant is a small village in the Bourne valley at the intersection of the A343 and the B3048. The entrance to the car park is at the eastern end of the village directly opposite the church (GR 385528).

By train: Whitchurch station is 3 miles from the route (if arriving by train, start the ride at St Mary Bourne).

Refreshments: There are pubs in all the villages except Linkenholt.

The route: Several challenging climbs in the mid-section of the route, otherwise easy.

Turn **L** from the track leading to the car park, passing the church on your right, to ride through Hurstbourne Tarrant. It is a beautiful village. Streamside cottages are linked to the road by small footbridges and beyond the village rise the steep wooded hillsides of the Bourne valley.

Just past the pub on the left you meet the A343. **Turn R** into The Square for just a few yards then **turn L**, signed

Vernham Dean, Ibthorpe and Upton. Continue for about ¼ mile to Ibthorpe. You will see Ibthorpe House, a fine 18th-century building, beyond a small green with a seat on your right. Jane Austen spent holidays here with her friends Martha and Mary Lloyd, and often walked with them in the hills.

Follow the road to a junction in Upton. Keep straight ahead, signed Vernham Dean. In the village, pass the pub on

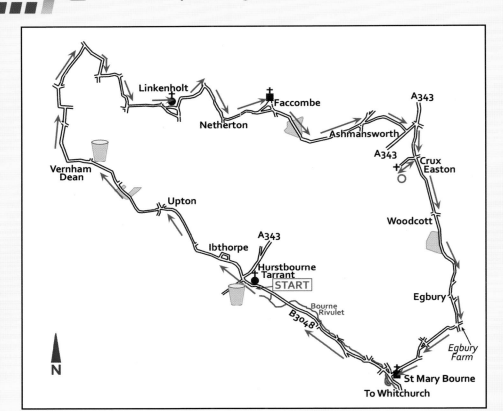

your right and keep straight on, signed Oxenwood and Hungerford. The road bends sharply right. **Turn immediately R** up the lane signed Henley and Buttermere. The lane winds uphill to a junction. Bear right, signed Buttermere, to a T-junction. **Turn R**, signed Vernham Street and Linkenholt, to follow the county boundary. On your left there are splendid views over the Wiltshire downs.

After ½ mile the lane curves right downhill then swings left, signed Vernham Street and Linkenholt, and continues to a junction. **Turn L**, signed Linkenholt. In ¾ mile you ride into this picturesque village, which seems lost in the hills. The church is on your

left. The arch of the small window just to the left of the porch is decorated with a row of 'shepherd's crowns', the local name for fossilised sea urchins found in the chalk.

At the T-junction **turn L**, signed Faccombe and Combe, to follow the road along the top of Cleve Hill Down. There is no hedge on your left and the views north, over miles of downland, are breathtaking. Continue to a T-junction and **turn R**, signed Netherton and Andover. The road runs downhill past Netherton House to a junction. **Turn L**, signed Faccombe. As you enter Faccombe **turn L** at the Y-junction to ride down to the church and see a little of this remote village.

Ibthorpe where Jane Austen visited Martha and Mary Lloyd

Turn R in front of the church to pass the large Georgian manor on your left and **turn L** at the Y-junction, signed Ashmansworth and Highclere.

A ride of 2 miles brings you to Ashmansworth, the highest medieval village on chalk in England. At the junction as you enter the village **turn L**, signed Newbury, and shortly after **turn R**, signed Hurstbourne and Andover. The lane runs for a mile to meet the A343. **Turn L**, signed Newbury and Highclere. After ¼ mile you will see a sign on the left indicating a lane on the right for Crux Easton, Woodcott and Egbury. Shortly after you come to the turning so **turn R** as directed.

Now you can enjoy the splendid

downhill run I mentioned in the introduction. After ¾ mile **turn R**, signed Crux Easton. After ¼ mile you will see the Crux Easton wind engine in a field on your left. Return to the road and **turn R** to resume the route of the tour, heading south. Keep straight on at the crossroads in Woodcott and continue straight ahead in Egbury (do not take the turning for St Mary Bourne on the right). After ¼ mile **turn R**, signed St Mary Bourne, passing Egbury Farm on your left. On your right, high embankments mark the site of a prehistoric camp known as Egbury Castle. At the junction follow the sign for St Mary Bourne and Whitchurch. Shortly after, at the T-junction, **turn R** for St Mary Bourne and follow the road downhill to the main street in the village, the B3048.

Crux Easton's 19th-century wind engine

Turn **R** to ride through the village and along the valley with the Bourne rivulet running through the meadows on your right. After 3½ miles you will see Hurstbourne Tarrant church. Turn **L** opposite the church to return to the car park.

HURSTBOURNE TARRANT

Today this small village could not look more peaceful but early in 1940, during the Second World War, the atmosphere must have been very different. To protect RAF Andover a decoy site was built in the area of the village in order to deceive enemy aircraft. The decoy airfield was made to look as realistic as possible with fake aircraft and buildings. The villagers must have passed many sleepless nights!

CRUX EASTON WIND ENGINE

The Crux Easton Wind Engine is a John Wallis Titt 'Simplex' self-regulating geared wind engine. It was erected for the Earl of Carnarvon in 1891 to pump water from a well 410 ft deep. It has a 20-ft wind wheel on a 32-ft hexagonal skeletal steel tower. The angle of its 48 canvas sails is adjustable to allow for variations in the strength of the wind. A fan tail enables the engine to turn into the wind. The pumped water supplied the manor house and the farm and the engine also drove a circular saw and a pair of millstones.

From April to August inclusive the Crux Easton Wind Engine is open to the public from 11 am to 4 pm on the second Sunday of the month.

13

White Hill and Watership Down

22 miles

Spectacular views are a feature of this splendid downland tour. A few miles north of the Test the downs rise to form a steep range of rounded hills, which descend dramatically in a series of combes and escarpments, giving breathtaking views over Berkshire and the Thames valley. The tour starts in Overton, an attractive village on the banks of the Test, and takes you across the downs to one of the best viewpoints, White Hill. This is a great place to stop for a picnic, listen to the larks and watch buzzards mewing and circling overhead. On the way you follow in the steps of the Roman legions along the Portway. There are more villages to explore including Hannington, one of Hampshire's gems. After a climb up Watership Down, familiar to all readers of Richard Adams' novel, a long, gentle descent brings you back to the Test valley.

Maps: OS Landranger 185 Winchester & Basingstoke and 174 Newbury & Wantage.

Starting point: Overton long-stay car park. From the centre of the village follow the signs for the long-stay car park off the B3400 by Turnpike Cottages (GR 520498).

By train: Overton station.

Refreshments: Pubs and restaurants in Overton. Pubs en route at Hannington and Freefolk.

The route: One stiff climb up Watership Down. The rest of the route is easy.

Turn L from the long-stay car park in Overton then **turn L** again along the B3400, heading east. After ¾ mile, at the crossroads, **turn L**, signed Ashe, North Oakley and Hannington. Shortly you will see Ashe House, a beautifully-proportioned Georgian property on your left.

Continue to go under the railway to a crossroads. Keep straight on, signed North Oakley and Hannington. The lane bears right through North Oakley

to a junction. **Turn L** for Hannington to ride past the pub into this lovely village of brick, flint and thatched houses, surrounding a wide green. The church overlooking the green dates back to Norman times. In front of the church an old wellhead is covered by a pointed roof erected in 1897 to commemorate Queen Victoria's Diamond Jubilee.

Leave the village heading north to a T-junction. **Turn L** (unsigned) to a

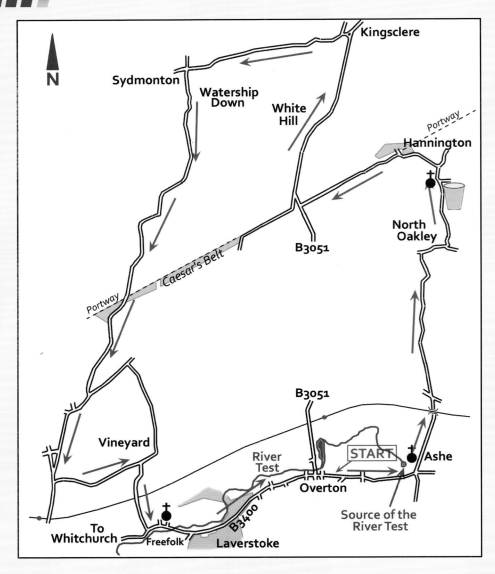

Y-junction. **Turn L** again to follow the lane along the line of the Portway, a Roman road that runs from London to Weymouth via Silchester, Old Sarum and Dorchester. After ¾ mile you leave the Portway when you meet the B3051. **Turn R**, signed Kingsclere, and after a few yards, at the junction, **turn R**

again, signed Kingsclere. The lane runs uphill past the Gallops on your left to bring you to White Hill to enjoy magnificent views. The downs have been inhabited since earliest times and close to the car park there is an ancient settlement.

Cottages at Freefolk village

Follow the lane downhill, heading for Kingsclere. As you enter the village **turn L**, signed Sydmonton and Old Burghclere, for just a few yards to a T-junction. **Turn L**, signed Sydmonton and Old Burghclere. Continue for 1¾ miles to the first turning on the left. **Turn L** to head south towards the heavily-wooded slopes of Watership Down.

Climb the Down and take a break at the top to enjoy the views. If you have read Adams' novel *Watership Down*, you will recognise some of the descriptions of the Down where the rabbits sought a new home. Richard Adams grew up in the area and knew it very well. He based his story on a collection of tales he told to his young children to pass the time on trips to the countryside.

Now you have your reward for the stiff climb – a downhill run of 3 miles. You cross the Portway once more, at the point where it is known as Caesar's Belt as it is bordered for over a mile by a ribbon of trees. At the T-junction **turn R**, signed Whitchurch. Continue for ¾ mile to another T-junction. **Turn L**, then almost immediately **turn L** again, signed Wooldings. After ¾ mile you need some careful navigation! On your left you will see the entrance gates to a vineyard. **Turn R** opposite the gates (the turning is unsigned but it is the first turning on the right).

The lane goes over the railway to meet the B3400. **Turn L** to ride through Freefolk, passing a charming row of thatched cottages on your left. Continue through Laverstoke, once famous as the home of Portals paper

Rolling downland on the way to White Hill

mills. In 1920 the business was moved to Overton. Laverstoke Park Farm is owned by Jody Scheckter, the 1979 Formula 1 World Drivers' Champion. He now follows a new career as an organic farmer and landowner.

Follow the B3400 through Overton village to the long-stay car park, which is on your left.

● ● ● ● ● ● ● ● ● ● ● ● ● ● ● ● ● ● ● ●

ASHE

Ashe House was the home of one of Jane Austen's closest friends, Mrs Lefroy. Here Jane met and possibly fell in love with an Irish nephew of Mrs Lefroy, Tom. Just how serious she was remains a mystery! Ashe church was rebuilt in 1877. At the eastern corner of the churchyard, a cross marks the grave of Lieutenant Robert Portal, of Her Majesty's 5th Royal Irish Lancers, one of the few survivors of the Charge of the Light Brigade at Balaclava.

HENRI DE PORTAL AND LAVERSTOKE

Laverstoke paper mills are still in the centre of the village behind high walls. There is a romantic story about the founder of the famous mills, Henri de Portal. Born in France, in order to escape religious persecution, it is believed he and his brother were hidden in wine casks and smuggled by faithful friends on board a lugger. They arrived safely in England and young Henri learned paper-making in Southampton. Energetic and enterprising, he took over Bere Mill near Whitchurch. His business prospered and in 1718 he leased the neighbouring mill at Laverstoke and eventually built another mill nearby. He started making the newly-invented watermarked bank note paper in 1724 and three years later he was awarded the privilege of making notes for the Bank of England. North-east of the mills, Laverstoke House was built for his descendants in 1790.

The Heart of Hampshire

21 miles

In the heart of the county, between the Test Valley and the little River Dever, there is some delightful pastoral countryside crossed by a network of grass-bordered lanes leading to farms and remote riverside villages. The tour explores this very special part of Hampshire and as there are no steep hills to negotiate it is ideal for everyone. The route begins in Micheldever, an enchanting village of deep-thatched, timber-framed houses. The village stands on the banks of the Dever, a sparkling chalk stream that runs west to meet the Test near Wherwell. From Micheldever you head north to Whitchurch where there is an opportunity to visit Britain's only working silk mill. Then you turn south to follow a lane meandering along the east bank of the Test, with beautiful views over the river. A lane through woods leads you south over the Dever to Barton Stacey, then heads east beside the river through Stoke Charity, an old-world village with a lake and picturesque cottages, to return to Micheldever.

Map: OS Landranger 185 Winchester & Basingstoke.

Starting point: The parking area opposite the church in Micheldever, a small village 6 miles north of Winchester (GR 513391).

By train: Micheldever station is on the route.

Refreshments: Pubs and restaurants in Whitchurch. Pubs in Barton Stacey and Wonston.

The route: Quiet lanes, undulating.

From the parking area opposite the church in Micheldever head north, leaving the church on your left, heading for Micheldever station. You pass Northbrook House on your left. The lane runs beside the railway embankment on your left. At the crossroads **turn L** over the railway then immediately **turn R**. Follow the lane as it bears left past the Dove Inn on the right to a T-junction. **Turn L** for just a few yards then **turn R**, signed for the A303, Andover and Whitchurch. Almost immediately bear right, following the lane under the A303, and continue ahead, following signs for Whitchurch and Laverstoke.

The lane runs through attractive countryside dotted with woodland. After 1 mile there is a sharp right-hand bend. Shortly after the bend **turn L** along an unsigned lane (the lane you are leaving is signed Laverstoke and

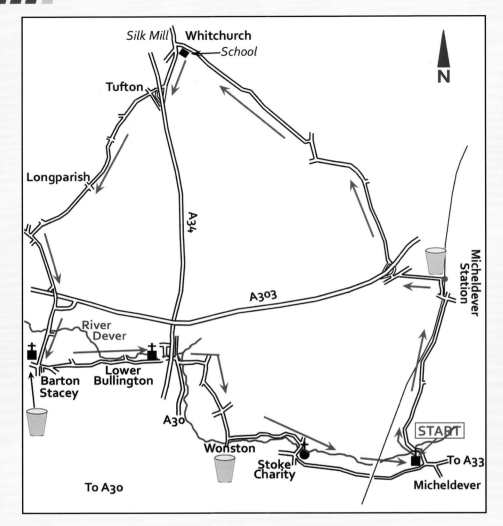

Overton). Although you have had no signs the lane does lead to Whitchurch! Just past the school on your left you reach a T-junction. If you would like to visit the mill, **turn R** for just a few yards to the lane on the left, with a brown sign for the Silk Mill. **Turn L** to follow the sign for the mill. There is a large car park with security bars where you can chain your bike. After your visit **turn R** from the entrance and

keep straight ahead. If you decide not to visit the mill **turn L** at the T-junction.

Keep straight ahead for ¾ mile then **turn R**, signed 'Tufton Local Traffic'. Go under the A34 and **turn R** (unsigned). Keep ahead over the weak bridge to a junction. As the road bends right, keep straight on down a narrow lane signed to Longparish. (This sign

Stoke Charity

may be partly obscured by bushes and it is very easy to miss this turning.) A beautiful lane leads you beside the Test straight over a crossroads and past the Fisheries to a T-junction. **Turn L** to cross the bridge over the A303 and keep straight on, following the signs for Barton Stacey.

The lane crosses the Dever to bring you into Barton Stacey. Opposite the church **turn L** into Bullington Lane, signed 'Bullington and Micheldever station'. Continue through the lovely Dever valley to Lower Bullington on the banks of the river, which is on your left. Just past the church you go under a high arch of the former Didcot, Newbury & Southampton railway. It was constructed in the 19th century to carry what was the Southampton to Didcot line.

Go under the A34 to a T-junction. **Turn R** for just a few yards then **turn L** for Norton. Cross the Dever and keep ahead to a T-junction. **Turn R**, signed Wonston. Go straight over the crossroads to return to the river in Wonston. **Turn L**, signed Hunton, just before the river bridge. The lane leads you beside the river, which is now on your right, to Stoke Charity. As the lane curves right to take you to the bridge over the Dever, there is a beautiful view of Stoke Charity church across the meadows on your left.

Ride into the centre of the village to a junction of several roads. Take the first road on the left, signed Micheldever, to

Stoke Charity church seen across the meadows

pass the church on your left. The lane follows the Dever valley to go under the railway and bring you back to Micheldever. **Turn L** at the junction to the parking area opposite the church.

● ●

WHITCHURCH

This attractive Georgian town, lying in a fold of the downs beside the Test, has been designated a Conservation Area because of the richness of its wildlife. As it runs through the town, the river widens into many small streams crossed by bridges, which make ideal places to pause and enjoy the peaceful atmosphere. But in earlier times the scene would have been very different! In the 13th century full use was made of water power, which worked four watermills, located every half mile along the river. The mills were used for grinding corn, finishing wool, weaving silk and dressing cloth. Today, only the silk mill has survived. The building stands on an island in the river and has been recently restored. It is a simple brick building, with large windows to allow as much light as possible for the looms many of which date from the late 19th century. Silk has been woven at the mill since 1830 and the waterwheel still turns. The mill produces high-quality silk to order. It is open from 10.30 am to 5 pm on Tuesday to Saturday; also Sundays in summer and bank holidays. Visit during the week if you can, to see work in progress.

The Enchanting Itchen Valley

22 miles

he River Itchen is one of Hampshire's treasures. For Charles Kingsley, a frequent guest at the Plough Inn in Itchen Abbas, it was 'the loveliest of vale rivers'. The sparkling water of this clear chalk stream inspired his book *The Water Babies*. Old-world villages with thatched roofs are dotted along the river valley, framed by wooded hillsides. Follow the route of this tour and I think you will agree with the famous author! The route starts north of the river on Abbotstone Down. You follow the River Alre south to Alresford where it meets the Itchen. The restored Mid-Hants Steam Railway runs from Alresford to Alton and you may like to take a nostalgic journey back into the age of steam. The route then crosses the downs east of Cheriton where, in 1644, the most decisive battle of the English Civil War was fought. South of Cheriton the tour makes a detour to discover the source of the Itchen before following the river through Cheriton and Tichborne, a historic village with a story to tell! Beautiful tree-lined lanes lead you along the south bank of the river, rising occasionally to give wide views over the valley. The tour crosses the river and heads north along peaceful downland roads to return to the car park on Abbotstone Down.

Map: OS Landranger 185 Winchester & Basingstoke.

Starting point: Abbotstone Down Hill Fort car park beside the B3046, 1½ miles north of Alresford (GR 584361).

By train: Alresford station is on the route.

Refreshments: Alresford offers good pubs and restaurants and the station buffet is open every day except Mondays. There are pubs in most of the villages beside the route.

The route: Quiet lanes over undulating downland and along the river valley.

Turn R from Abbotstone Down Hill Fort car park along the B3046. Keep to the main road, signed Alresford. Continue through Old Alresford.

Ride up New Alresford High Street to a T-junction. **Turn L**, signed Alton and Ropley. Go under the railway bridge, heading for Bishop's Sutton. When you see the Ship pub ahead, **turn R** just before you come to the pub (the turn is unsigned but it is the first turning on the right). Almost immediately **turn L** up Scrubbs Lane. Continue under the main road to a Y-junction, where you bear left. The lane leads to a small green facing the shallow valley where the Battle of Cheriton was fought in

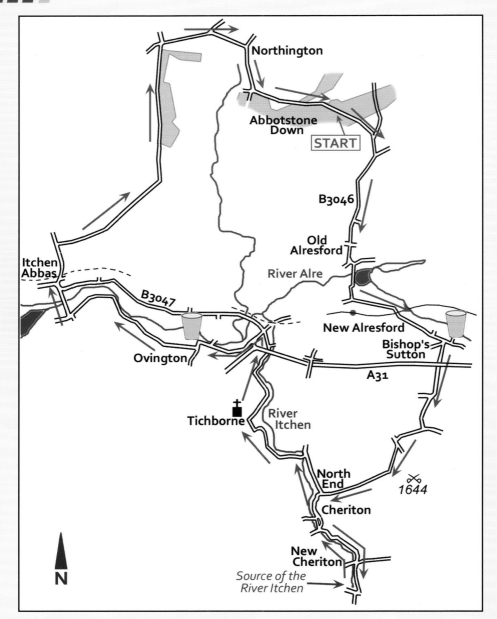

the Civil War. There is an information board giving details of the battle and a memorial to the 2,000 men who lost their lives. **Turn R** to ride along the ridge where the Cavaliers assembled before the battle.

After 1½ miles you enter Cheriton

Crossing the downs to Cheriton

village and meet a T-junction at North End. The route continues by turning right at this point but I suggest you make a short detour to ride through Cheriton and discover the source of the Itchen. So **turn L** at the T-junction. Cheriton is a delectable village, threaded by a network of streams flowing through lawns and under bridges. At the next T-junction **turn L**. The stream is on your right. Go straight over the crossroads into Kilmeston Road. You come to some white railings either side of the lane. Beside the railings on your right a post with a yellow arrow marks the start of the Itchen Way. Looking over the railings, I could see springs bubbling into a small pond. This is supposedly the source of the Itchen but there are other possible springs in this marshy area.

Return to North End and continue heading north for ¼ mile to a junction. **Turn L**, signed Tichborne, and follow the road into the village. Tichborne church, which dates from the 11th century, should not be missed! **Turn L** up Church Lane. The church has its original door with an iron sanctuary ring, a Saxon chancel with splayed windows and beautifully-carved Jacobean pews like small rooms.

The lane continues under the main road to a crossroads. Some careful navigation is needed now! **Turn L**. You will see an island ahead. Just before you reach it **turn R**, signed Ovington. As you approach the village you will see a pub on your right. **Turn sharp L** over a bridge and after a few yards **turn R**. There is a blue cycleway sign on the corner.

Now you enjoy a lovely riverside ride for 1¼ miles. Just before the village sign for Avington **turn R** (unsigned). You pass the gates to Avington House, once a favourite resort for Charles II and Nell Gwynne, on your left. Cross the river to meet the B3047 at Itchen Abbas. **Turn L**, signed Kings Worthy and Winchester, for just a few yards to

The Civil War memorial on the downs near Cheriton

a Y-junction. **Turn R**, signed 'Veterinary Centre and School'. Go under a railway bridge and continue to a crossroads. **Turn R** (unsigned) and continue for 2¼ miles to a crossroads. **Turn R**, signed Northington and Alresford, to a Y-junction. Bear right, signed Northington Only, to meet the B3046. **Turn R**, signed Alresford. The road leads over Abbotstone Down past a car park to your car park on the right.

● ●

OLD ALRESFORD

Old Alresford is a village of quiet charm. Many of the houses, dating from the 17th and 18th centuries, overlook wide greens shaded by majestic trees. In the 12th century Bishop de Lucy built a causeway over the Alre to his New Market, now known as New Alresford. The causeway also served as a dam, creating Old Alresford Pond, which you will see on your left from the route. Originally it provided power for corn and fulling mills and fish for the bishop's table. Now it is a haven for wildlife.

THE MID-HANTS STEAM RAILWAY

The railway earned the name 'the Watercress Line' as one of its main functions was to transport this perishable crop from the River Alre where watercress flourished in the clear chalk streams. The headquarters of the restored line is in New Alresford. The Information Office and West Country Buffet are situated on Platform 1 and there is a picnic area overlooking the station. For information, telephone: 01962 733810.

THE TICHBORNE DOLE

The origins of the Tichborne Dole date from the 12th century. On her deathbed Lady Mabella begged her husband to give the value of a small part of their land to the poor. He offered her as much land as she could crawl round carrying a burning brand. She encircled 23 acres, still known as 'The Crawls'. Each Lady Day, 25th March, the villagers gather at Tichborne House to collect their 'Dole': 7lbs of flour for each adult and half as much for each child.

Quiet Lanes in the Western Downs

20 miles

The South Downs reach their most westerly point a few miles south of Winchester. This is a splendid tour following tranquil lanes winding over the western downland through remote countryside, dotted with farms and hamlets. As you cycle along these remarkably peaceful lanes, you really feel you are in a different world, far away from the noise and bustle of the 21st century. On my last ride in these hills I was hardly surprised to see two roe deer calmly walking up the lane towards me! The route starts in Bishop's Waltham, a historic market town at the foot of the western Downs. As you head north from the town you are soon in glorious countryside, with wide views over rolling hills and steep-sided valleys. Past the tiny hamlet at Lane End you turn east towards the lower slopes of Beacon Hill. On the way you reach Beacon Hill National Nature Reserve, an ideal place to pause and admire the views from one of its many vantage points. Then you have a change of scene as the route runs downhill into the Meon valley to Exton, a beautiful riverside village. You follow the eastern bank of the river through Meonstoke, another attractive village, before heading west along the Dundridge valley to return to Bishop's Waltham.

Map: OS Landranger 185 Winchester & Basingstoke.

Starting point: Lower Lane long-stay car park, Bishop's Waltham (GR 554177).

By train: No convenient station.

Refreshments: Bishop's Waltham has delightful pubs and restaurants. There is a pub by the route ¾ mile east of Lane End, and at Exton and Dundridge.

The route: Moderately challenging.

Turn **L** from the entrance to Lower Lane car park to meet the B3035. **Turn R** and keep straight on to a junction. Leave the B3035 and **turn L** at Beeches Hill, signed Cheriton and Alresford. Continue to a T-junction at the top of the hill and **turn R**. Keep ahead for ¾ mile. **Turn L**, signed Upham and Owslebury. After only 100 yards **turn R** along an unsigned lane.

After 1 mile you come to a T-junction. **Turn R** and keep straight ahead, following the sign for Longwood Dean and Winchester. At the Y-junction, bear right over Blackdown. Go straight over the next crossroads, signed Longwood Dean. You now follow a beautiful winding lane beneath an arch of coppiced trees. You leave the trees to continue along a ridge, with wide valley views.

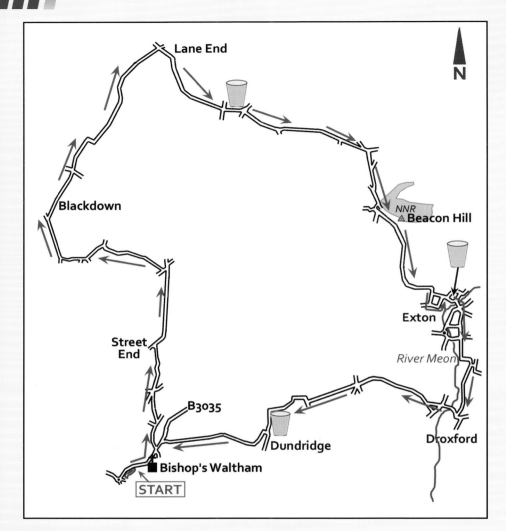

Turn R at the T-junction at Lane End, signed Preshaw and West Meon. After 1 mile go straight over the crossroads, signed Preshaw, Warnford and West Meon. (If you would like a break, there is a pub on the left.) Keep straight on over crossroads following signs for Warnford and West Meon. The view towards Beacon Hill is breathtaking! After 1 mile you reach a lane on your right, which is your way. Unfortunately

when I was last here the signpost was broken. Look for the name 'Rooks Green' on the circle on the top of the signpost and **turn R**. Do not worry if you miss this turn as 300 yards further on there is another lane on the right you can take, signed Droxford and Swanmore.

Follow the lane downhill to Beacon Hill National Nature Reserve. After

St Peter's Street, Bishop's Waltham

turning right at the entrance to the Reserve, the main road turns sharply left at a junction. A few yards after this, as the road bends right again, keep straight ahead down a narrow single-track lane. This lane has a warning notice forbidding heavy goods vehicles from using it, despite instructions from their Satellite Navigation Systems to the contrary! The lane runs steeply downhill into the Meon valley and turns sharply left then right to a junction. Keep straight on, signed Exton. At the T- junction **turn L** along Allans Farm Lane. The lane turns left to a T-junction. **Turn R** to a junction by the pub. **Turn R** to cross the bridge over the Meon. Go over the A32 to Stocks Lane and after 100 yards **turn R** along Rectory Lane. Keep straight on at a grass triangle, following the

sign for Droxford and Soberton. Continue along Meonstoke High Street, a charming village street, lined with creeper-covered Georgian houses.

The road bears left into Chapel Road, then right, still following the east bank of the Meon, to bring you to a T-junction. **Turn R**, signed Droxford and Corhampton. Cross the Meon and go straight over the A32, signed Dundridge and Sheep Pond Lane. Keep ahead to go over a main road, following the sign for Dundridge Down. The lane winds along the Dundridge valley past the woods of Dundridge Nature Reserve to a junction by a pub. **Turn R**, signed B. Waltham. Continue, to meet the B3035. **Turn L** and keep ahead for 300 yards, then

Meonstoke village

turn L into Lower Lane to your car park, which is on your right.

• • • • • • • • • • • • • • • • • • • •

BISHOP'S WALTHAM

Bishop's Waltham is an enchanting small town, with many gabled 16th- and 17th-century houses, as well as elegant Georgian dwellings. The High Street is ideal for window shopping, retaining many small local businesses, as well as some traditional and specialist shops. St Peter's Street, with its charming Georgian cottages, leads up to the church, which dates from the Norman Conquest.

In medieval times the bishops of Winchester were rich and powerful and in 1136 Bishop Henry de Blois built the now ruined palace. Much of what you see today is the work of William Wykeham, Bishop of Winchester in the mid-14th century. The palace also welcomed royal visitors. Here Henry V prepared for Agincourt and Queen Mary Tudor waited for King Philip of Spain to arrive for their wedding. Cromwell ordered the palace to be destroyed in 1644 but there are extensive remains to explore. These include a corner of a range of buildings that provided lodging for guests. The ground floor now houses Bishop's Waltham Town Museum; open late March to the end of October, 10 am to 6 pm. Telephone: 01489 892460.

BEACON HILL NATIONAL NATURE RESERVE

Today a great deal of the downland is farmed but some areas of chalk grassland remain, particularly on the steeper slopes. Some of these areas are now protected as nature reserves. The reserve at Beacon Hill is noted for its wildflowers, which include rock roses, yellow rattle and several varieties of orchids. These attract a host of butterflies. Among them you may spot the Chalkhill Blue and the Silver-spotted Skipper.

Hambledon and the Meon Valley

17 miles

Rolling downland, a lush river valley and a forgotten railway all feature in this exciting tour in the south-east of the county. The lovely village of Wickham is your starting point. Markets and fairs are held in the huge central square, which is surrounded by attractive shops, elegant Georgian houses and gabled cottages, many of which date from the 16th century. From the car park on the site of the former station the route heads east over Wickham Common before turning north to take you along quiet country lanes to Hambledon, an old-world village tucked so snugly in a fold of the downs that it looks as if it has grown there! From Hambledon you head west, following remote lanes rambling over low hills to Droxford in the beautiful Meon valley. Now you have a choice of routes. If you wish, you can follow the Meon Valley Railway Trail to return to Wickham, a distance of about 4 miles, or you can ride along the valley, following the attractive lanes close to the track, which I describe below.

Maps: OS Landranger 196 The Solent & Isle of Wight and 185 Winchester & Basingstoke.

Starting point: The free car park on the site of the former station in Wickham (GR 576117).

By train: There is no railway station close to the route.

Refreshments: Good pubs and restaurants in Wickham. Pubs on the route include those at Hipley, Hambledon, Brockbridge and Soberton. Lotts Tea Room near Hambledon is ideal for cyclists, with plenty of room outside for your bike and inside for you.

Turn L from Station Close and after 180 yards **turn L** again into Bridge Street, the B2177. Cross the A32 and keep straight on along Southwick Road, passing the church on your left. Keep ahead, passing pleasantly wooded countryside, through North Boarhunt to a crossroads. Leave the B2177 here and **turn L**, signed Denmead. After ½ mile **turn L**, signed Hambledon and Soberton. Pass Hipley Copse on your

right to reach a Y-junction. **Turn R**, signed Denmead and Hambledon and follow the well-signed road towards Hambledon.

The lane runs along a valley lined with small, thickly-hedged fields and paddocks framed by wooded hillsides. When you meet the B2150 **turn L**, signed Droxford, Clanfield and Hambledon, and ride towards

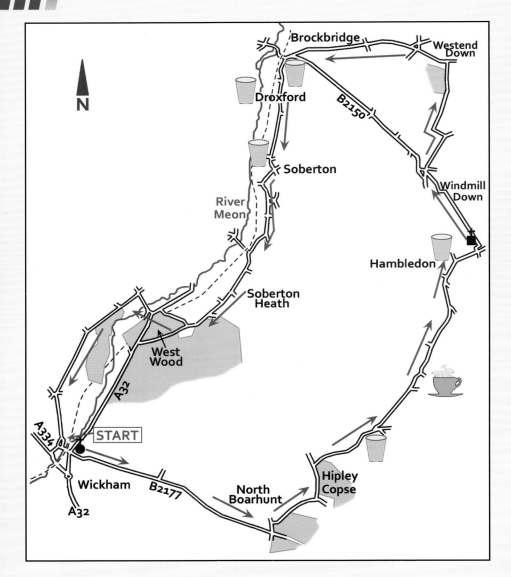

Hambledon village. On your left you pass Lotts Tea Room, popular with all cyclists! At the Y-junction **turn R**, signed Clanfield and Petersfield, to ride through the village. After only ¼ mile **turn L** up the road towards the church. **Turn R** in front of the church then almost immediately

turn L, leaving the church on your left.

The lane crosses the lower slopes of Windmill Down to a T-junction. **Turn R** and go straight over the crossroads, following the sign for Chidden and East Meon. In ¾ mile at

Lott's Tea Room, an ideal refreshment break

the T-junction **turn L**. After 200 yards **turn R** (the first lane on your right) to follow the lane running a little uphill to a T-junction on Westend Down. **Turn L**, signed Droxford and Meonstoke. Continue straight on over the crossroads. The lane runs high with glorious views before dropping into the Meon valley and meeting the B2150. **Turn R** for a few yards then **turn L**, following the sign for Soberton, passing the Hurdles pub on your left. After a few yards you will see Droxford station house, now private, on your right.

Continue along the road to Soberton for ¼ mile to a bridleway sign on your right. *If you would like to ride the Railway Trail to return to Wickham* **turn R** and follow the bridleway to a bridge over the track. Just before the bridge, wheel your bike down the narrow path on the right, which leads down to the track. **Turn L** to follow the Trail, which

brings you back to the car park in Wickham.

If you prefer to return to Wickham along the lanes, continue along the road past the bridleway sign to the crossroads in Soberton. **Turn R**, signed Soberton Heath, Newtown and Southwick. When you reach the Y-junction by the war memorial **turn R**, signed Soberton Heath, Swanmore and Bishop's Waltham. At the next junction **turn L**, signed Soberton Heath and Newtown. Keep ahead along Heath Road through the village of Soberton Heath to a Y-junction. **Turn R**, signed Swanmore and Curdridge.

The lane leads to the A32. **Turn L**, signed Wickham and Fareham, then almost immediately **turn R**, signed Swanmore and Curdridge. Go over the Meon to a crossroads. **Turn L**, signed Wickham and Titchfield. At the

The Meon river near Droxford

Y-junction **turn L** and at the next junction **turn L** again to ride into Wickham. Keep straight on and **turn L** along Station Close to return to your car.

● ● ● ● ● ● ● ● ● ● ● ● ● ● ● ● ● ● ● ●

HAMBLEDON

Allow time to explore Hambledon. All the houses are charming, many concealing half-timbered walls behind the rounded bow windows and pedimented doorways of Georgian days. The street up to the church is particularly attractive with cobbled pavements and colourful gardens. The church of St Peter and St Paul was built around a little Saxon church, which still forms part of the nave.

MEON VALLEY RAILWAY TRAIL

The railway through Droxford from Alton and Fareham opened in 1903. A plaque beneath the post box records a significant event in Droxford's history. During the Second World War, early in June 1944, Sir Winston Churchill and his War Cabinet met other war leaders in a special train at Droxford station to plan the D-Day Normandy landings. The railway closed for passengers in 1955, and in 1962 it was closed for goods traffic. Now the route forms the Meon Valley Railway Trail, following the trackbed of the former railway from West Meon south to just beyond Wickham.

ROYAL FOREST OF BERE

The Royal Forest of Bere once stretched from the River Test at King's Somborne in the west through Hursley, Bishop's Waltham and Denmead to Rowland's Castle in the east. Many of the small forested areas you pass on this tour were once included in the boundary of the Royal Forest.

18
The South Downs

17 miles

Y ou do not have to travel far in Hampshire to discover splendid cycling country. A few miles north of the county's bustling seaports, within sight of the sea, rise the South Downs, a beautiful range of hills threaded by narrow country lanes. Follow the route of this tour to enjoy the special timeless appeal of these chalk downs. The ride starts in Buriton, an attractive village with a pond alive with ducks. From the village, a scenic road leads you through the heart of the Queen Elizabeth Country Park. Then you climb the downs to one of the highlights of this tour, Butser Ancient Farm. This is a real working Iron Age farm with thatched roundhouses and authentic animals and crops. Then, a highlight for all cricket fans – cycling past Broadhalfpenny Down, famous as the home of the Hambledon Cricket Club that dominated the world of cricket in the 18th century. There is also an opportunity to visit the lovely village of East Meon, with its Norman church and medieval Court Room, before you take quiet country lanes to return to Buriton.

Maps: OS Landranger 197 Chichester & The Downs and 185 Winchester & Basingstoke.

Starting point: Buriton car park. From the south, leave the A3 for Petersfield and follow the signed lane to Buriton. From the north, leave Petersfield on the B2070 and turn left down the signed lane to Buriton. Drive down the High Street to the car park by the pond (GR 740200).

By train: Petersfield station is 3 miles north of Buriton.

Refreshments: Café in the Queen Elizabeth Country Park and several pubs on the route.

The route: Some climbs but generally undulating.

Turn L from the car park by the pond in Buriton and ride up the High Street. Just past the pub on your right **turn L**, signed Chalton and Finchdean. Go under the railway arch and continue uphill, keeping straight on for Chalton. On either side of the road rise the heavily-wooded slopes of the Queen Elizabeth Forest. After 2 miles the railway runs close to the road and shortly after this you come to a T-junction. **Turn sharp R** and follow the road to a T-junction in Chalton village. **Turn R**, signed Clanfield and Petersfield.

After ½ mile you come to the entrance to Butser Ancient Farm on your left. A

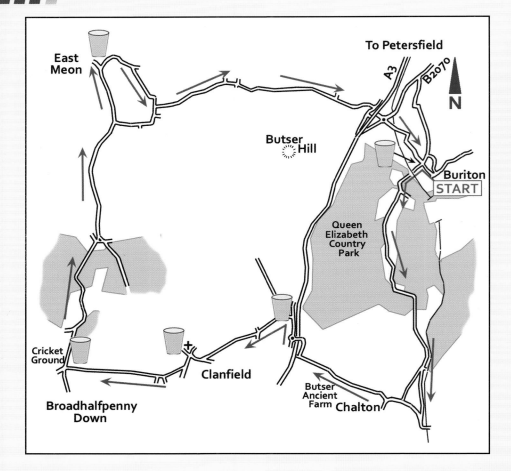

visit to the farm is a 'must'! Then continue up the road towards the A3. Just before the A3 you meet a minor road. **Turn R** for Clanfield. The road curves left over the A3 to a roundabout. Do not at this point turn left for Clanfield (although you are going to the village) but **turn R**, signed London and Petersfield. Just past the Hampshire Hog pub **turn L**, signed Butser Hill (Country Park) up Petersfield Lane. As you approach the village **turn R** at the T-junction, signed Hambledon and East Meon, and a few yards further on you come to a

junction in the village in front of the Rising Sun Inn. **Turn L**. The church and the thatched well-house (reminiscent perhaps of a Iron Age roundhouse?) are on your right.

Pass the church and at the next junction **turn R**, signed Hambledon. Continue for ¾ mile to a crossroads by the Bat and Ball pub. **Turn R** along Hyden Farm Lane, signed East Meon. On your left is Broadhalfpenny Down. The monument on the corner commemorates the great days of the Hambledon Cricket Club. The road

Butser Ancient Farm

leads through woodland and goes over a crossroads.

You now enjoy a wonderful downhill swoop with glorious views as you head for East Meon. Ignore the sign for Buriton on the right. As you approach the village you need some careful navigation. At the Y-junction **turn R**, signed Frogmore (the sign may be slightly obscured). The route then follows the lane away from East Meon village. But if you prefer to explore this historic village before continuing the route, keep straight on at the Y-junction.

Follow Frogmore Lane as it curves left over a stream then heads south for ½ mile to a junction. **Turn L**, signed Buriton and Ramsdean. Keep straight on along Ramsdean Lane. You are surrounded by the rounded wooded hillsides of the downs, rising on your right to their highest point at Butser Hill.

The road runs under the A3 to a roundabout. Follow the signs straight ahead for Buriton. The lane leads for ½ mile to the village. Ride down the High Street to the car park by the pond.

● ●

THE QUEEN ELIZABETH COUNTRY PARK

The park, which covers more than 1,000 acres of dramatic scenery ranging from high open downland to steep thickly wooded hillsides, provides opportunities for many outdoor activities. The visitor centre has an audio-visual theatre, a craft centre and a well-stocked shop. Refreshments are available in the Coach House Café. The park is open daily. The visitor centre and café are open from March to October inclusive from

Hambledon Cricket Club memorial stone on Broadhalfpenny Down, with the Bat and Ball pub behind

10 am to 5.30 pm, and the rest of the year from 10 am to 4.30 pm. Telephone: 02392 595040.

BUTSER ANCIENT FARM

The farm brings to life the Iron Age, which lasted from around 800 BC to the coming of the Romans in AD 43. Most of the land in southern Britain was under the management of efficient and practical farmers and today the farm is cared for in much the same way. Friendly and enthusiastic staff are ready to chat and answer questions at any time. The farm is open on a 'drop in' basis every day from Easter to the beginning of October from 10 am to 5 pm, and for the rest of the year weekdays only. Telephone: 02392 598838.

CLANFIELD

The church of St James is built on the site of a medieval church. The bells hung in

the open belfry tower have survived from this earlier building. The well was the community's only source of water for many years. Once this small village was much larger and was a royal manor. After the Norman Conquest it was given to Roger Montgomery who led the vanguard of William's army at the Battle of Hastings.

BROADHALFPENNY DOWN

For nearly thirty years the Hambledon Club made their headquarters in the hospitable Bat and Ball pub and beat the Rest of England in a series of matches for enormous wagers watched by huge crowds. They established and refined the laws of cricket and among their improvements was the addition of a third stump! Today the Down is the home of the Broadhalfpenny Brigands Cricket Club.

Jane Austen's Hampshire

27 miles

This tour in the north-east of the county, south of Basingstoke, takes you through the rich pastoral landscape that formed the background to Jane Austen's novels. If she was to walk, or jog in her donkey cart, along the leafy lanes today, she would still find the peaceful world that inspired her writing. So I have started this circuit close to her house in Chawton. After a visit to Jane's home you ride north past Alton to South Warnborough. Then you head west to Upton Grey, one of Hampshire's most attractive villages, with a pond surrounded by old timber-framed cottages. From the village you follow the valley of the River Whitewater to Greywell beside the Basingstoke Canal. There is a ride along the towpath of the canal for 1½ miles before you reach Colt Hill Bridge close to Odiham Wharf. Lanes winding through remote countryside and sleepy villages lead you back to Chawton.

Map: OS Landranger 186 Aldershot, Guildford & surrounding area.

Starting point: The public car park behind the car park for the Greyfriars pub in Chawton opposite Jane Austen's house (GR 709375).

By train: Alton station is close to the route.

Refreshments: Cassandra's Cup teashop by the car park provides delicious meals. There are pubs in most of the villages.

The route: Mostly easy, some gentle climbs.

Turn R from the car park opposite Jane Austen's house. The road curves right to a T-junction. **Turn L**, signed Alton, along the A339 to go under the A31. The open green on your right is The Butts. In the past most villages had butts where, from an early age, men had to practise shooting with the longbow in order to develop strong back muscles in readiness for war. Keep straight on under the railway to a T-junction. **Turn R** along the B3349, signed Odiham.

After ¼ mile, at the traffic island, turn **L** signed Odiham, still following the B3349. Continue heading north along a wide green valley. Go straight over the crossroads at Golden Pot and keep ahead towards South Warnborough. Pass the South Warnborough village sign and as you enter the village **ignore the turning on the left leading uphill, signed Upton Grey** (this has fallen into disuse). Keep ahead to a second turning on the left, just beyond the church, signed for Upton Grey and now **turn L** for the village.

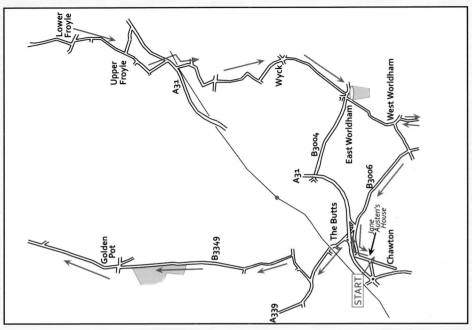

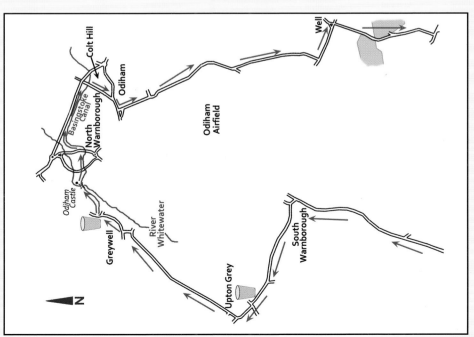

Jane Austen's house at Chawton

The lane leads to a T-junction by a phone box. **Turn L** (unsigned) to ride into Upton Grey. The novelist Henry Fielding set a rather doubtful scene in *Tom Jones* in the local pub, the Hoddington Arms! **Turn R** by the pond, signed Tunworth and Mapledurwell. Pass the church to a Y-junction in front of a small letterbox and a broken signpost. **Turn R** (unsigned). A lovely ride brings you to a T-junction. **Turn R**, signed North Warnborough, to ride through Greywell village. Although so close to a motorway this tiny village remains peaceful and unspoilt. The village street, bordered by a single row of houses and cottages, many timber-framed, overlooks meadows sloping down to the River Whitewater.

Pass the Fox and Goose pub on your left and **turn R** for a few yards down Deptford Lane. Wheel your bike up the footpath on your left, which brings you down to the Basingstoke Canal towpath by the Greywell Tunnel. In 1932 part of the tunnel collapsed and it now houses the largest bat roost in Britain.

Continue along the canal towpath. Just after the canal crosses the River Whitewater you will see the ruined keep of Odiham Castle on your left. This romantic ruin is all that remains of a castle built by King John in 1207. From here he rode out to set his seal on the Magna Carta at Runnymede.

The canal curves right to run under two road bridges and after ¾ mile you reach Colt Hill Bridge. Ride under the bridge and look back at the arch to check the name. **Turn L** up the bank to the road and **turn L** again up Colt Hill to a T-junction in Odiham. **Turn R.** Keep ahead for 300 yards then **turn L**, signed Long Sutton, Cricket Club and Bridewell. Keep straight on at a junction, passing Odiham Airfield on your right. RAF Odiham is the home of the Royal Air Force's heavy lift helicopter, the Chinook.

The enchanting village of Upton Grey

At the next T-junction **turn L**, signed Well. It comes as no surprise when, just before a crossroads, you come to an ancient well surmounted by a canopy erected to commemorate Queen Victoria's Silver Jubilee. **Turn R**, signed Lower Froyle. As you approach the village you come to a T-junction. **Turn L** for a few yards then **turn R** (unsigned) along a lane, which brings you to Upper Froyle. At the far end of the village **turn L** at the junction. The lane leads to a service road in front of the A31. Bear right along the service road for a few yards, then cross the road. **Turn R**, signed Winchester and Alton.

Continue for only 200 yards then **turn L**, signed Wyck. Go straight over the crossroads and keep straight on in Wyck for East Worldham. As you come into East Worldham you pass some oast houses on your right. Hop growing was once a major industry in this part of Hampshire. At the T-junction **turn R** then almost immediately **turn L** past the pub for West Worldham. At the Y-junction in West Worldham **turn R**, signed Alton, to meet the B3006. **Turn R** for Alton and at the junction **turn L**, signed Chawton, to return to the car park.

JANE AUSTEN AT CHAWTON

Jane was thirty-three when she moved into Chawton Cottage, as the house was then called, with her widowed mother, sister Cassandra and close family friend Martha Lloyd. After several years with no settled home she could once again enjoy the happy, useful life she loved, surrounded by the Hampshire countryside that was her home. By the window in the living room you can see the small table at which she sat to revise her earlier novels, *Sense and Sensibility* and *Pride and Prejudice*, and write the great novels of her maturity *Mansfield Park*, *Emma* and *Persuasion*. The house is open daily in June, July and August from 10 am to 5 pm; other months until 4.30 pm. January and February open weekends only. Telephone: 01420 83262.

THE BASINGSTOKE CANAL

The canal was completed in 1794 to increase the prosperity of the area by transporting timber and agricultural produce from the flourishing market town of Basingstoke to London via the Wey Navigation. After falling into disuse, restoration work began in 1973 and today it provides a beautiful waterway rich in plants and wildlife.

Where Romans Trod

22 miles

The north of the county, east of the Downs, is splendid cycling country. A network of grass-bordered lanes spreads over undulating countryside dotted with patches of ancient forest. Small villages surround wide greens and commons. People have settled here from the earliest times and left their mark. In the first century AD the Roman legions came and founded Calleva Atrebatum on the site of an Iron Age fort near present-day Silchester. Calleva became the administrative capital of the area and an important trading centre. The tour explores some of the countryside crossed by three Roman roads on their way from Calleva, south to Winchester, east to London and west to Salisbury. If you feel like a break from the Romans, the route runs through Pamber Forest with a wealth of tempting footpaths. It also passes The Vyne, a 16th-century mansion now owned by the National Trust, and the great house of Stratfield Saye, the gift of a grateful nation to the Duke of Wellington after his victory at Waterloo.

Map: OS Landranger 175 Reading & Windsor.

Starting point: The large car park at Silchester Roman town. From Silchester follow the brown signs for the Roman town (GR 637628). NB: The entrance to the car park has a height restriction barrier. There is room outside to take your bikes off your car, if necessary.

By train: Bramley station is on the route.

Refreshments: Several good pubs on the route. Restaurant at The Vyne, tearooms at Stratfield Saye.

The route: Pleasantly undulating, no steep hills.

Before starting the tour you might like to follow the footpath from the car park and walk round the walls of the Roman town. The site is now grassed over but the thick walls are still impressive.

For the ride, **turn L** from the car park to a junction. **Turn L**, signed Silchester and Tadley. At the next junction continue left along Little London Road, signed Silchester and Little London. Keep straight on, passing a large green on your right, through part of Pamber Forest. Pass the pub in Little London on your right and continue to a T-junction. **Turn R** to meet the A340. **Turn R** for a few yards then **turn L**, signed Ramsdell and Charter Alley.

At the next junction **turn L**, signed Charter Alley and Ramsdell. The road

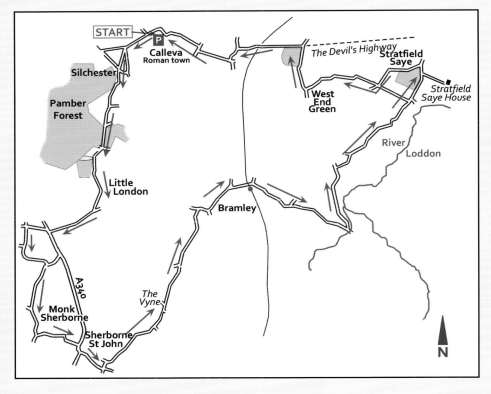

curves left to a junction. **Turn R**, signed Monk Sherborne. This is a splendid ride along unfenced grass-banked lanes to a junction. **Turn L**, signed Sherborne St John. Ride through the village to a T-junction. **Turn L**, signed Sherborne St John and Basingstoke, to meet the A340. **Turn R**, signed Sherborne St John and Basingstoke, for 400 yards then **turn L** along Cranes Road, signed Village Centre.

Ride through Sherborne St John to a T-junction. **Turn L**, signed Bramley, to a junction. **Turn R**, signed Bramley and follow the road heading north past The Vyne on your left. The visitor car park is further along the road on your left. After a visit continue along your route, heading north to a T-junction. **Turn R**, signed Bramley Station and Sherfield-on-Loddon. Keep to the main road to go over the level crossing and keep ahead, signed Sherfield-on-Loddon.

Now for some tricky navigation! Keep ahead until you see the Sherfield-on-Loddon village sign. **Turn L** just before the sign (no road sign). Continue heading north until you see a sign for Stratfield Saye. Just past the sign **turn R** along a second unsigned lane. This leads to a T-junction. **Turn R** along another unsigned lane and keep straight on past a lane on the left, followed shortly by a lane on your right. Continue to the approach to Stratfield Saye House, which is on your

St Mary's church built inside the walls of the Roman town of Silchester

right. You have a fine view of the house from the road.

After a visit **turn R** to resume the route, heading north to a T-junction. **Turn L**, signed Stratfield Saye and Bramley. The road curves left to a crossroads. **Turn R**, signed Silchester and Mortimer. The road now heads west to a T-junction in West End Green. **Turn R**, signed Stratfield and Mortimer. You are now riding north to meet the Roman road that heads east from Calleva through Staines to London. It is known as the Devil's Highway. Is that how the native Celts regarded the Roman invaders one wonders? **Turn L** along the Devil's Highway, signed Silchester. Go over the railway bridge to a T-junction. **Turn L**

(unsigned) to a T-junction. **Turn R** to meet the lane just east of the walls of Calleva. **Turn R** to follow the lane, which swings left to bring you back to your car park, which is on the left.

CALLEVA ATREBATUM – SILCHESTER ROMAN TOWN

Before the coming of the Romans, a local Iron Age tribe – the Atrebates – had a settlement on this site. The Romans developed it into a walled town, which became known as Calleva Atrebatum, the capital of the Atrebates. The town was laid out in a grid pattern with the forum in the centre surrounded by the public buildings and shops. Excavations have discovered the remains of temples, baths,

The 16th-century Vyne

small houses and a tiny Christian church dating from the 4th century. At present it is the only Christian church known to have been built during the Roman occupation.

THE VYNE

This elegant house was built for Lord Sandys, King Henry VIII's Lord Chamberlain. Later it passed to the Chute family who bequeathed it to the National Trust in 1958. Among many impressive features are the classical portico on the north front, a splendid staircase and an

exquisite Tudor chapel. Opening times vary. Telephone: 01256 883858.

STRATFIELD SAYE

The house dates from the early 17th century. The library was the Duke of Wellington's favourite room and has changed little since his day. The walls of the drawing room are hung with Dutch and Flemish paintings captured from Bonaparte's baggage-train after he was defeated at the Battle of Vittoria in 1813. Opening times vary. Telephone: 01256 882694.